T0031307

Veg Out

Veg Out

A Stress-Free Guide to Creating Your First Vegetable Garden

HEATHER RODINO

UNION
SQUARE
& CO.

NEW YORK

UNION
SQUARE
& CO.

NEW YORK

UNION SQUARE & CO. and the distinctive Union Square & Co.
logo are trademarks of Sterling Publishing Co., Inc.

Union Square & Co., LLC, is a subsidiary of Sterling Publishing Co., Inc.

Text © 2023 Heather Rodino

All rights reserved. No part of this publication may be reproduced,
stored in a retrieval system, or transmitted in any form or by any means
(including electronic, mechanical, photocopying, recording, or otherwise)
without prior written permission from the publisher.

ISBN 978-1-4549-4480-5
ISBN 978-1-4549-4525-3 (e-book)

For information about custom editions, special sales, and premium purchases,
please contact specialsales@unionsquareandco.com.

Manufactured in China

2 4 6 8 10 9 7 5 3 1

unionsquareandco.com

Cover photographs: Sarah Jun (*front*) © Union Square and Co., LLC;
Hero Images on Offset/Shutterstock.com (*back*)

Interior image credits on page 176

CONTENTS

PART TWO
PLANT PROFILES 75

INTRODUCTION

A vegetable garden is meant to be eaten. This simple truth can be easy to lose sight of in the course of the planning, digging, transplanting, watering, weeding, and mulching that are an inevitable part of the gardening process.

Unlike growing houseplants or other ornamental plants, this is a practical sort of gardening. But don't let the word *practical* put you off. There's just as much pleasure in it, maybe even more, because of the wonder in both the process and the product. The products of your garden will enrich your cooking, fuel and strengthen your body, and surprise your taste buds. If you love food, you'll find that nothing tastes as good as the literal fruits of your labor. You're feeding yourself and the ones you love, and along the way, you're experiencing the joy of tending and watching something grow. There's something special about that.

Your vegetable garden can be anything you like. It will most likely be a supplement to what you buy, but you may also wish, ambitiously, to grow everything you eat. It's a worthy goal, but don't let the perfect be the enemy of the good. I've found that with many things in life, it's best to start small, and the garden is definitely one of those things.

Some of my most indelible childhood memories involve the garden. When I was growing up, my mom kept a huge plot, and I had my own small garden within it. I remember the intense odor of tomato plants as I brushed against their leaves and the feeling of squeezing through rows of sweet corn, taller than I was, to harvest the cobs, which we'd then husk on the front porch over a stockpot, fighting with the cornsilk that stuck to everything. There were prickly raspberry bushes, their irritating qualities somehow intensified by the summer heat, and the sheer abundance of raspberry jam, frozen raspberries, raspberry bars, and so on, that made me grow tired of this favorite fruit—until

Veg Out

one day, in early adulthood, I tasted a raspberry at the Union Square Greenmarket in New York City and was transported back (yes, like Proust's madeleine), and began to love raspberries again. There were also dusky Concord grapes whose thick, tart skins and sweet, gelatinous interiors were nothing like what the supermarket considered a grape. Baked into crumb-topped pies, they were a symbol of the fall garden. Maybe you have similar memories or motivations for feeding yourself and your loved ones. Or maybe you're completely new to gardening. In either case, I hope this book helps you bring wonderful new flavors to your family's plates.

Your reason for starting a garden might be one of many: a desire to reduce your carbon footprint, a love of food or cooking, a craving for the freshest and tastiest ingredients, a way of increasing food security (especially in the wake of supply-chain issues or other disruptions), or as a hobby that takes you outside and away from life's other stresses. Or all of the above. Here are some of the most popular reasons people are drawn to vegetable gardening.

Take your meals to the next level.

You've probably heard this so often, it's become a cliché, but it's true: the food you grow tastes so much better than anything you can buy in a supermarket. Garden-fresh ingredients need little adornment. Think of a crunchy cucumber sprinkled with flaky salt, or a juicy tomato drizzled with a little olive oil and scattered with torn basil leaves, or crisp-tender green beans tossed in a Dijon vinaigrette.

Eat more plants.

Whether you're an omnivore, a vegetarian, or a vegan, we can all do better by eating more plants for our health and the health of the planet. When you have a garden, you'll find that eating more plants is almost irresistible because *you grew them yourself*.

Be happier and more connected.

Gardening has been shown to have mental health benefits and is sometimes even prescribed for people with anxiety, PTSD, or depression. Plus, it helps you connect more with your community—after all, you're going to have to give all that extra zucchini to someone. Why not the neighbor you usually only wave to?

Have food security.

At the onset of the COVID-19 pandemic in 2020, seed sales skyrocketed, as first-time and veteran gardeners alike wanted to grow food at home because of supermarket shortages, supply-chain issues, or simply to limit trips out to reduce their risk of contracting the virus. At the time of this writing, while the virus moves toward becoming endemic, shortages persist, and inflation and other concerns are still motivating people to grow their own food.

Regardless of your own motivations for gardening, you can't beat the convenience of having the ingredients you need for that must-make recipe just a few steps away, saving you a trip to the store for a tiny, overpriced plastic packet of limp tarragon or faded thyme.

Attract wildlife.

By gardening thoughtfully and organically, you can increase biodiversity in your own small but important way. Bees, beneficial insects, and other creatures will find their way to your garden. I've included a few wildlife-attracting plants in the profiles.

This book will walk you through the steps of starting your first vegetable garden, from selecting a spot for your garden and navigating seed catalogs to dealing with pests and harvesting your first crops. Along the way, I'll offer easy-to-understand guidance to try to reduce any feelings of frustration or intimidation and to help you succeed. If you've read my last book, *How to Houseplant*, you'll find that my goal is the same here: to streamline vegetable gardening so that you have the tools you need to get started and feel excited and empowered to do so, but not to overcomplicate the process and leave you feeling overwhelmed and drowning in information that's difficult to prioritize. You'll find that you'll naturally graduate to the next level as your interest and experience grow, and you'll learn how to troubleshoot and look for the answers you need. Remember that gardening is always a learning process.

PART ONE

THE BASICS

Even though you can learn the basics of gardening from books, YouTube videos, or TV shows, what really makes you a gardener is your own experience of gardening. It takes practice and a willingness to learn from your environment—as well as from your successes and failures. As British horticulturist Monty Don has written, "There's no one true way. If it works for you, then you are doing it right." There's a bit of finding your own way in the garden. As you become more experienced, your instincts will sharpen. You'll understand the growth cycle of each plant and know when something doesn't look or feel right.

Before you get started, it's worthwhile to first do a bit of groundwork and planning, such as deciding where to put the garden, how you're going to garden—in raised beds or in the ground—what type of soil you have, how long your growing season is, and what you want to grow.

Your Growing Season

The length of your growing season will vary greatly depending on where you live and the dates of the first and last frosts. Someone who lives in Maine, for example, has a much shorter growing season than someone who lives in Florida. Regardless of where you live in the world, you'll need to determine this piece of information locally. Check with a local extension office or horticultural society—or, if you're in the US or Canada, visit the *Old Farmer's Almanac* page at www.almanac.com/gardening/frostdates. Soil temperature is also important, because some seeds won't germinate in cold soil, will germinate very slowly, or will even rot.

If you have a short growing season, crops that take longer to mature may not be a good choice for you. There are ways to extend your growing season, such as starting seeds indoors (see page 44) and choosing varieties that mature faster. You can also use row covers and mulch to help warm the soil at the beginning of the growing season and to hold in warmth at the end of it. Cold frames and greenhouses are other options, but given that this is a book for beginners, we're going to keep things simple and work with the seasons. As you advance in skill and interest, you can look into some of these more advanced options. Although many of the plants you'll want to grow can't handle a frost, the good news is that there are some that can (and, in fact, some are even tastier after a frost, such as kale, page 118; carrots, page 96; and cabbage, page 92).

By contrast, if you live in a hot climate with a long growing season, you may be able to grow cool-weather crops by adjusting the traditional seasons and growing in off times such as fall or winter.

Your Place in the Sun: Deciding Where to Put Your Garden

One of the most important decisions you'll make is where to put your garden. Plants need sun, water, soil, and airflow to grow well, so you'll look for a sweet spot that contains the best combination of those factors.

Sun

Your ideal garden location should receive six or more hours of direct sunlight per day. Some plants will be fine with less, but you want to ensure that you choose the sunniest spot available. Watch out for trees; they will not only block sunlight, but their roots may extend into your garden area, limiting the usable space. Try to observe the light in season, because the angle of light changes throughout the year. (You may have noticed this in your own home when the angle of light is lower in winter.)

Water

Unfortunately, Mother Nature will not always cooperate and give you rain exactly when you need it, so you'll want to place your garden within easy distance of a water source. Water is heavy, so chances are, you don't want to be hauling full watering cans a long distance. Instead, make sure the location is within reach of a hose and at a comfortable distance from your tools and equipment. Finally, avoid low-lying areas prone to flooding—the last thing you want is for your garden to turn into a muddy swimming pool when it rains.

Soil

Soil is a gardener's most precious resource. If you're planning on growing in the ground (versus in a raised bed or in containers), you'll want to evaluate the kind of soil you have (whether it's rich and loamy, heavy with clay, rocky, or sandy with quick drainage). We'll spend a bit more time on this topic soon (see page 17). If you can, plant on a mostly flat surface to avoid erosion.

Airflow

Ideally, choose a spot that has good airflow. It helps plants grow and reduces the incidence of diseases and pests. Good airflow does not mean wind tunnel; avoid areas that are prone to incessant, strong wind currents.

What's that you say? You don't have 100 percent perfect conditions? Don't worry—almost no one does. We'll muddle through it together and troubleshoot as we go!

I Dig It! Raised Beds, In-Ground Planting, or Containers

One of the most important decisions you'll make after choosing where to put your garden is *how* you want to garden. There are pros and cons to each method, and only you can say what's going to work best for you. For most people, raised beds will be the style of choice, because in-ground planting relies on so many other variables. Urban dwellers, unless they are lucky enough to have a small backyard or access to a community garden, will need to rely on containers.

Raised Beds

A raised bed is a separated, boxed-in plot of earth dedicated to gardening. The soil's surface (the level at which you will plant the seeds) is higher than the surrounding ground (hence the term "raised"). Raised beds can be big or small—it all depends on your goals—and are usually rectangular in shape. A typical raised bed is no more than 4 feet (1.2 m) wide so you can reach in from any side without actually stepping into the bed. It's placed on top of the ground and filled with 6 to 12 inches (15 to 30 cm) of soil, sort of like a flowerpot with no bottom.

PROS

You're impatient. While there are no quick wins in gardening, raised beds do offer significant advantages to the gardener, since they provide a relatively controlled environment for your crops. For instance, a raised bed doesn't require you to improve your soil if it's heavy, sandy, or has other issues—a process that can take years and has its limitations. Instead, you directly control what goes into your beds. Choose quality soil (see page 17) that is aerated and drains well, and your crops will almost certainly be better off than if you gamble by planting in whatever soil happens to be around you. In other words, raised beds provide an excellent blank canvas for getting started on your gardening journey.

You want easier maintenance. When gardening, weeds come with the territory. Even though raised beds are not meant to be fortresses protecting your crops and keeping bad weeds at bay, they do reduce the incidence of weeds. Also, given that you won't be walking on the beds and compacting the soil (as you would in an in-ground garden, for example), the soil will be looser and thus any weeds will be much easier to pluck out. Another advantage is that because they are elevated, raised beds lift the work area closer to you, a bonus if kneeling or bending over for long periods of time is not for you.

You just want to get started already. The soil in raised beds will warm up faster than the ground; this allows you to start your growing season earlier. However, if you live in a warm climate, keep in mind that the raised bed will likely need increased irrigation throughout the growing season.

You want to make the most of a small space. If you have a limited space for gardening and want to make the most efficient use of that area, a raised bed can help you do so.

You want to make pest management easier. Accept it now: your garden is going to attract pests, but by building raised beds you can make it harder for some of them to eat your veggies before you do. Because a raised bed is a limited, confined space, it's easier to add physical barriers, such as row covers or fencing to protect the goodies the pests crave. It's also easier for you to monitor and control.

You want something that looks great! Simply put, a raised bed looks neat and organized, thereby adding aesthetic value to your property.

$$$. Unless you have a source of free quality soil, you'll need to purchase the soil that will go in the bed and the compost you will need to enrich it. This cost can vary substantially depending on the materials you choose, for example, whether you decide to go with bags from a garden center or to have it delivered in bulk (which may be more economical). There's also the cost of the materials to build the raised beds to consider, which could vary from around fifty dollars if you go completely DIY to a hundred dollars or more for a kit.

The initial work. While in the end a raised bed will make gardening easier and more efficient, up front you'll need to put in some labor in building it and in moving the soil. A kit might make things easier if you're not so handy, but the cost of that will be higher. If you're really not into this aspect of things, you might perhaps be able to bribe some of your handier friends or relatives to help you build it with the promise of a share of your harvest later on—or at least a few pizzas.

Increased watering. As mentioned above, a raised bed typically dries out faster than an in-ground garden (a raised bed has better drainage), so you may need to water more often, particularly if you live in a hotter, drier location.

Not perfect for all crops. Some crops, like corn, require larger areas because of their pollination needs. Other plants, because of their size, will need to be trellised to grow well in a raised bed.

In-Ground Planting

In-ground planting is exactly what the name says. You're going to grow directly in the soil you've got.

Veg Out

PROS

¢. By far, this is the most budget-friendly option. You don't need to pay for soil to fill a bed, and you don't need to build anything. You don't have to put in as much labor to get started either.

Less permanent. If you're on the fence about this whole gardening thing or you're feeling like you just want to try something in a small area and see how it goes, in-ground planting may be for you, especially if you've got good soil. You can also move your garden to a new location later on if you discover that the spot you've chosen isn't working for you.

Reduced irrigation. An in-ground garden won't dry out as fast as a raised bed, so you won't be watering as much during the growing season.

CONS

Soil challenges. If you've got rocky or heavy soil, your growing conditions will be more challenging. You can improve things to an extent over the course of several years with compost and mulch, but you'll always need to work within the limits of what you've got. This may mean smaller crop yields, which in turn may force you to be a little pickier about what you grow, based on what you observe grows well. By far, this may be the biggest disadvantage of in-ground gardening. Soil quality may also be a concern, especially in urban environments, which is why a soil test (see page 19) that specifically checks for contamination (in addition to providing general information on soil composition) is recommended.

Weed challenges. As noted above, an in-ground garden will have more weeds competing with your plants for sun, nutrients, and space. Weeds can also harbor pests. Mulching can help reduce weeds (see no-dig gardening on page 29), but with an in-ground garden you'll need to be more vigilant for weeds than with a raised bed.

More pests and diseases. You'll also have more competition for your harvest from pests that burrow or simply walk or crawl right into your garden.

Accessibility issues. If you don't want or are not able to work down at ground level because of back, knee, or other issues, in-ground gardening might not be the best choice. Always be honest with yourself about what you're able and willing to do; otherwise, your garden may transform from a fun endeavor into a dreaded chore.

Containers

If you are an urban dweller, don't have space for a garden, just want to dip your toe into gardening, or simply don't find an in-ground garden or raised beds appealing, containers are your answer. You can grow almost anything in the right size container, and many plants that require a lot of space to grow have compact varieties that grow well in containers. Some weedy plants, like mint, are actually better grown in containers because they tend to take over the garden otherwise.

PROS

Space saving. A container garden can be as big or small as you like. You can have a handful of pots of herbs ready to clip fresh for whatever recipe you're making that night, or you can fill big whiskey barrels with larger plants such as cucumbers and tomatoes, or you can do both! You can also get creative about the kinds of containers you use; potatoes, for example, can be planted in grow bags.

Moveable. You can place your containers in the best spot to receive the sunlight they need, and if the weather suddenly turns harsh (say, a midsummer hailstorm), you can move the containers to a sheltered location.

Easy start-up and less planning. For sure, many people find the idea of preparing the ground for a garden or building and filling a raised bed quite daunting, and these types of gardening also require nontrivial investments of time, money, and labor. But grabbing a few pots and bags of soil at your neighborhood garden store is easy and (relatively) inexpensive. Container gardening is versatile and manageable, and thus it can be a way of gauging your interest to see if you really enjoy growing your own fruits and vegetables.

Watering. Pots can dry out quickly, and you'll want to make sure that you stay on top of watering. For some plants, drying out even once can be detrimental (but so can overwatering, so always check the soil first to see if it really needs it), and stressed plants are more prone to disease and pests. On really hot days, you may have to water some plants more than once a day.

Fertilizing. Plants can quickly exhaust the nutrients present in the soil in a container, so you'll want to keep up with their fertilizing needs, which will vary by plant.

Cost. You'll need to buy potting soil to fill the containers, and while this is obviously much cheaper than filling a raised bed, it's still an up-front cost that can add up. It's very likely that you'll find yourself going to the garden store repeatedly to buy soil, too, since you'll be replacing much of the soil in the containers after each growing season. While you can reuse some of the soil from a pot that grew a healthy plant, you should refresh it with at least 50 percent fresh soil, because over time, the quality declines as the soil breaks down and nutrients are lost. If the plant had any problems with pests or disease, discard all the soil. Also, the "return on investment" of container gardening is lower: unless you have a massive container garden, you won't have the same yield as you would from an in-ground or raised-bed garden, and if you're really unlucky, you may even end up with exceedingly tiny yields that will hardly make a dent in your typical produce needs.

Limited varieties. While you can grow most anything in a container, you'll need to be savvy and choose dwarf or bush varieties of plants, which will stay more compact. Although the focus of this book is on traditional gardening, whenever possible, I'll suggest varieties suitable for containers.

Here's a secret: You don't have to choose a single gardening method. You can do one or both or all three, depending on your space, your plants' needs, and your goals. You could grow sweet corn in the ground, most of your veggies in a raised bed, and herbs and hot peppers in a handful of pots by your doorstep.

From the Ground Up: Determining Soil Quality

Ask any longtime gardener what the most important part of a successful garden is, and they'll say the soil. While you can't change the kind of soil you have if you're growing your vegetables in the ground, you can improve it over time with organic matter, such as compost. How do you determine what kind of soil you have? Let's grab a handful and take a look.

Clay. Clay soil is heavy and sticky, and when it's wet, its small particles will easily squeeze together and you'll be able to roll it into a ball. Clay has a lot of nutrients, but it doesn't drain well or have good aeration. When it dries, as it would in periods of drought, it becomes very hard. While most crops like soil that is more free draining than clay, in the short term you can focus on crops that need more moisture, like brassicas and lettuce, and incorporate plenty of compost to improve drainage.

Sand. Sandy soil feels gritty, like, well, sand, and when it's dry it will run through your fingers. Its large particles drain well, but the soil is poor in nutrients. Mediterranean herbs, such as lavender and rosemary, grow well in sandy soil, as does lettuce, beets, and carrots.

Silt. Silty soil is in between sand and clay. It has medium particles and a good amount of nutrients, feels somewhat slippery, and compacts easily when wet but not to the same degree as clay. Even though it drains well, silty soil can easily wash away. Like clay, silty soil needs organic matter added to it, but also as with clay, you can grow brassicas, lettuce, corn, and other shallow-rooted crops in it.

Loam. Considered the ideal type of soil for vegetable gardening, loamy soil is a well-balanced mixture of clay, silt, and sand. It contains small, medium, and large particles, which gives it the benefits of all three soils—good drainage, sufficient water retention, aeration, and nutrition—with few of the downsides.

Very few people have "perfect" soil, and even those who have loamy soil benefit from adding organic matter to improve its structure and boost its fertility.

Soil and the pH Factor

In evaluating your soil, especially if you're doing it for the first time, you should have at least a passing familiarity with pH. A measure of acidity or alkalinity, pH falls on a scale of 0 to 14. A pH of 0 would be the most acidic (hydrochloric acid is one example), and a pH of 14 would be the most alkaline (sodium hydroxide, for example, a chemical found in liquid drain cleaners). A pH of 7 is neutral. Most soil is on the slightly acidic side, with a pH falling somewhere between 5.5 and 7. This range is good for gardening, though some crops prefer it slightly more acidic or slightly more alkaline. (Blueberries, for example, are well known for their acidic soil needs.)

To determine the composition of your soil, you can get it tested at a soil laboratory or local extension office. This inexpensive test will also give you a good indication not only of pH but of the nutrients present in the soil. (Note: If you're also concerned about potential soil contaminants, such as heavy metals, the lab may offer an option to test for them for an additional fee.)

If you just want a quick indicator of pH, though, follow this fun tip from *The Old Farmer's Almanac Vegetable Gardener's Handbook*. It will take you back to those baking soda and vinegar volcanoes you made as a child. Place a few tablespoons of soil in a bowl and stir in ½ cup distilled white vinegar. If the mixture fizzes, the soil is alkaline. If not, move on to the next test: Place a few more tablespoons of soil in a separate bowl and moisten it with distilled water. Stir in ½ cup baking soda. If it fizzes, the soil is acidic. If it doesn't fizz with either baking soda or vinegar, the soil has a neutral pH.

Over time, adding good compost (see page 20) will help correct pH issues, but you can also add lime to make the soil more alkaline and sulfur to make the soil more acidic.

The Cleverness of Compost

Composting is one of the best things you can do to boost soil health and plant health. It's also a natural form of recycling, which reduces organic waste in the household, thereby limiting what ends up in the landfill. Bacteria, microbes, fungi, and worms break down the organic matter and convert it into a crumbly, sweet-smelling substance that gardeners call black gold.

Because composting takes time and a bit of space, when you're first starting out, you may prefer to buy it, but it's a good idea to start your own pile as soon as possible. This process can be as easy or complex as you want it to be, but I recommend a purpose-built composting bin, which is a good choice for a small garden and helps you get going quickly. You can also start a compost pile on the ground somewhere in the yard, or you can go big from the start and use recycled wooden pallets to build a series of bins or enclosures to speed up the process.

As you start learning more about composting, you'll hear the terms "browns" and "greens." These refer to the kinds of material that comprise the compost pile.

Browns: shredded, dry leaves; straw; cardboard (cut up, if possible); pine needles; wood chips; newspaper; sawdust

Greens: fruit and vegetable scraps; uncooked kitchen waste; coffee grounds; grass clippings

A good guideline is that the ratio of browns to greens should be roughly 50:50, and the smaller the pieces, the greater the surface area, so the material will break down faster. It's better, however, to err on the side of more browns than greens. Compost needs oxygen, so once a month or so, turn the pile over. If it's wet and smells bad, add brown materials.

Some materials shouldn't be thrown into the compost pile. Meat, fish, and dairy products may attract vermin. Don't add diseased plants, pet waste, or anything treated with chemicals, such as pesticides and herbicides.

Much Ado About Mulch

There's one myth about mulch that we need to bust right away. When you think "mulch," the first thing that may come to mind may be wood chips, but mulch doesn't have to mean wood chips—not at all. Mulch is simply a layer of (usually) organic matter spread on top of the soil. It helps reduce moisture loss, reduces erosion, regulates soil temperature, suppresses weeds, and improves the structure of the soil, adding nutrients as it breaks down. It also makes a garden look nice and neat, and you can add mulch even if you're growing in containers. Mulch should be spread in a layer at least 2 inches (5 cm) deep on your raised bed or in-ground garden. Your choice of mulch (see next page) may depend on making the most of what's plentiful and easily accessible in your area.

Black plastic. Black plastic mulch can have certain uses, such as to suppress weeds or to warm up the soil. It's also easy to find and use, but it's not very eco-friendly, so I recommend limiting its role in the garden.

Compost. Compost is an ideal mulch because it's nutrient-rich, moderates pH, increases microbial activity, and much more, but you may not have enough of it to spread thickly over your garden, so mix and match it with other options.

Hay. Hay and straw are different things. Hay is a grass and plant unto itself, while straw is a by-product. Hay breaks down faster than straw, thereby releasing its nutrients into the soil more quickly. However, hay often contains seed heads, which can then sprout into annoying weeds. That being said, some gardeners find that weeds from hay are not that hard to control and are generally worth the benefit the hay offers. You may also be able to find seedless hay in some areas.

Leaf mulch/mold. Rake up those fall leaves and save them, either for your compost pile or to mulch your garden. For best results, shred them and let them break down over the winter before adding them to your garden the following spring.

Straw. Straw is the stalk left over after harvesting grain crops. It's lightweight and a great choice for composting and mulching (strawberries, anyone?), especially in warm climates, though it takes a while to break down. You can also use straw to bulk up raised beds.

Wood chips. Wood chips can be used as mulch, but with a few caveats. Avoid anything that has been dyed (hint: nothing red!) or treated. Source the wood chips carefully: obtain them from a reputable supplier (or shred them from your own waste wood) and place them in a pile until they start to break down before adding them to your garden. (The smaller the pieces, the more quickly they will decompose.) Also keep in mind that wood chips can acidify your soil.

Raise Your Raised-Bed IQ

Size matters. A raised bed should be no more than 4 feet (1.2 m) across so that you can reach in from either side without stepping on the soil, which compacts it, and anywhere from 8 to 10 feet (2.4 to 3 m) long. Why that length? Any longer, and you'll be tempted to walk on the soil, or you'll find it inconvenient to walk all the way around. Twelve inches (30 cm) is a good height to shoot for, but the walls can be higher or lower, depending on what's comfortable for you. (Keep in mind that a higher bed requires more soil to fill, but it may be the way to go if you have mobility issues.)

Choose your materials carefully. You can purchase raised bed kits if you're not handy. If you're building your own from scratch, opt for a wood that resists rot, such as cedar, redwood, oak, or cypress. Avoid chemically treated wood and railroad ties, which are treated with creosote. Concrete blocks, stone, and composite lumber are other options for your raised bed.

Level the surface. Use a level to see if the surface of the ground where you want to place the bed is flat. If not, you'll want to remove some of the soil until it is.

Consider spacing. If you're building more than one bed, make sure to leave enough space between the beds so that garden equipment, such as a wheelbarrow, will fit through them.

Cover it up. To help suppress weeds, line the inside of your bed with cardboard before you add soil. When the cardboard breaks down, it will also nourish the soil. This is especially important if you're building a bed that is shallower than 12 inches (30 cm), where weeds are more likely to break through. Now you've got a use for all those boxes that might normally end up in the trash or recycling—just remove any labels, tape, or staples before adding the cardboard to your bed.

Calculate what you need. Soil is typically measured in cubic feet or yards. To calculate your soil needs, multiply the length of the bed by its width and its height. For example, for a standard bed, 8 feet long (2.4 m) × 4 feet wide (1.2 m) × 1 foot high (0.3 m) = 32 cubic feet (0.9 m) of soil.

Fill 'er up. When it comes time to fill your bed, you have a few options. You can use a 50:50 mix of garden soil and compost. Or you can use a mix of topsoil, coconut coir (as a substitute for peat moss, which is no longer recommended due to sustainability issues), compost, and other amendments such as perlite or vermiculite to improve drainage. Ideally, you should finish the bed with a 2-inch (5 cm) layer of compost. A landscaping company or local nursery may offer more affordable options for larger quantities of soil than buying lots of bagged soil at a big-box store, but find out what's in the soil before purchasing it, so you can be sure it's high quality.

In-Ground Gardening

If you're opting for the in-ground route, there are two approaches to consider to prepare the earth for your garden.

Tilling

The most conventional approach for starting a garden would be to first mark out the area and clear the grass, digging up any weeds and their roots. A tiller—which you can rent from a big-box home improvement store, or perhaps borrow from a neighbor—loosens, turns, and aerates the soil, breaking up big clumps. Tilling should be done on dry soil, not wet. As you till, you'll want to pick up any remaining clumps of grass and toss them on your compost pile.

If you've done a soil pH test, here's where the results can come in handy because now's the time to incorporate any amendments, such as lime or fertilizer. Add a thick layer of compost (at least 2 inches/5 cm), then rake the surface to even it out and break up smaller clumps. You might want to wait at

least a few days (or up to a few weeks) after tilling the soil to plant because it gives the soil time to incorporate the amendments; waiting also allows the soil's microorganisms, which have been disrupted, to restabilize. In the meantime, you can add a layer of black plastic mulch (see page 22) or landscaping fabric to prevent weeds from coming back as well as to reduce soil erosion.

No Dig

While tilling the soil has its benefits, it also has its drawbacks. According to the University of New Hampshire Extension, tilling "weakens the soil's microbial community that metabolizes and holds nutrients, sequesters and holds carbon, and absorbs and holds water. . . . Tilled soil is still bacterial rich, but un-tilled garden soil is also rich in fungi. Fungi help your plants become more productive, and your garden will be more productive without disrupting the fungal community within your garden's soil." In addition, while tilling can be beneficial for starting a new garden plot and reducing weeds, it also surfaces dormant weed seeds that may germinate and grow.

No-dig or no-till methods, by contrast, use a layer of light-excluding mulch (typically cardboard boxes) on top of the undisturbed soil and a layer of organic matter, ideally compost, over the cardboard. Leaf mulch and well-rotted (not fresh) manure are other good options. Without light, anything that lies under the cardboard will not be able to grow. This method does not require any fancy equipment, leaves the soil microorganisms and fungi intact, and essentially builds a rich layer of compost on top of your soil. Over time, as the cardboard breaks down, small weeds will get through, but you should be able to easily remove them. Just repeat the process of mulching until the weeds have exhausted themselves. Again, make sure to remove any tape, labels, or staples from your cardboard before using it. Be aware that this method does take some time and may require several applications, but many gardeners swear by it.

For more on this method, check out the work of Charles Dowding, who has written several books on the subject and maintains an active website and YouTube channel.

Dream a Little Dream: Seed Catalogs

Now that you've determined where and how you're going to garden, the fun part begins: deciding what you're going to plant. For established gardeners in the Northern Hemisphere, the arrival of seed catalogs in January and February is a moment of excitement. This annual ritual is a confirmation that winter will indeed end and that the growing season is just around the corner. Seed catalogs are a gardener's candy shop, sparking the imagination and making it nearly impossible not to order all the things. Some catalogs are quite functional in design, while others are beautifully laid out, almost like a book, or even hand-illustrated. If you've never gardened before, you will be blown away by the available variety of vegetables and herbs from around the world: Japanese turnips, Ethiopian kale, Italian beets, Taiwanese long beans. Imagine dozens of peppers and chiles, endless salad greens, and pages and pages and pages (and pages) of tomatoes—cherry, paste, heirloom, hybrid, dwarf. . . . In one recent seed catalog, I counted four pages of basil, with more than twenty-four different choices.

Seed catalogs are invaluable resources themselves, providing critical growing information, descriptions of plant varieties, and, often, photos. Indeed, you might find yourself hanging on to them as you would a reference book—and best of all, they're free. Seed companies will vary by country, but in the United States, Baker Creek Heirloom Seeds, Kitazawa Seed Company, Johnny's Selected Seeds, Southern Exposure Seed Exchange, and Renee's Garden are a few places to start.

It's okay to let yourself get a little carried away envisioning all the incredible dishes you will turn out with these options—it will open your mind to what's possible—but first let's take a step back and plan the garden!

Planning the Garden Plot

In deciding what to plant, when, and where, we'll take into account three things: cool- and warm-weather crops, succession planting, and crop rotation. Let's talk about each of these in turn. While it may sound a bit like a game of *Tetris*, trying to figure out what goes where and when, in practice, it's actually much easier than it sounds.

Working with the Seasons: Cool- and Warm-Season Crops

Although a greater consciousness of eating with the seasons has developed over the past fifteen years or so, many of us are still divorced from the concept of seasonal food. We expect to buy tomatoes, peas, peaches, and strawberries year-round, despite the limited seasonality of each. It's a familiar refrain, one you've probably heard many times before. If you shop at farmers' markets, though, you may be more primed to the seasons—the surprise of asparagus's first appearance, the first delicate baby greens, the stubborn persistence of apples and pears and root vegetables. Similarly, when you start to garden, you'll become increasingly attuned to the rhythms of the seasons and better understand what grows and when.

Most crops can be roughly divided into either cool- or warm-season crops. (Some, however, are sort of in between, like potatoes, and others can grow throughout most of the year.) You'll first plant the cool-weather crops, followed by the warm-weather crops. For example, you won't be harvesting lettuce or spinach on the hottest days of summer (unless your summers are very cool), so those are planted first, and you can't grow tomatoes in most places in the spring, so those are planted later. This planting rhythm will help you make efficient use of limited space.

Because different crops will go into the ground at different times, it's very important to determine the length of your growing season (see page 6) and know the average highs and lows throughout that season. For example, if your summer temperatures are routinely in the 90s (around 30°C) and you don't start your tomato plants early enough, the blossoms might scorch and drop before they can set fruit.

If you live somewhere cold, with a short growing season, you can start crops indoors to get a head start. You can also choose quicker-maturing varieties—those wonderful seed catalogs come in handy here, because they indicate the period to maturity. Also, check out local nurseries and regional seed companies, which will likely specialize in varieties that grow well in your area.

If you live in a warm location, particularly in areas that don't receive frost, your window for growing cool-weather crops may be very small, and it's worth seeking out heat-tolerant varieties of other crops to make the most of your climate. Plants can be shielded from the hottest sun with shade cloth.

The chart that follows lists common cool- and warm-growing garden herbs and vegetables.

Cool-Season Plants

Arugula	Dill
Beets	Kale
Broccoli	Lettuce
Cabbage	Parsley
Cabbage, Chinese (Napa)	Peas
Carrots	Radishes
Cilantro	Spinach
Collard greens	Swiss chard

Warm-Season Plants

Amaranth	Garlic
Basil	Lavender
Beans	Oregano
Borage	Peppers/chiles
Corn	Pumpkin/winter squash
Cucumbers	Sweet potatoes
Edamame	Tomatoes
Eggplant	Zucchini

Write It Down

It's a good idea to keep a garden journal to track what you plant, how well it grows, what the harvest was like, any problems or issues you had along the way, and so on. This can take any form you like: a dedicated notebook, a Word document, or even a spreadsheet—whatever works best for you. A garden journal is also useful for keeping track not only of what you planted but also where and when you planted it; the time and location are worth recording so that you can rotate your crops (see page 35). You might find it helpful to sketch a simple garden, scaled to the dimensions of your plot, so you can place what needs to go where and when. In this way, journaling can also help you decide what to grow (and where and when to grow it) in the future.

It's Just One Thing After Another: Succession Planting

With succession planting, you sow small quantities of the same crop periodically for a continuous harvest rather than all at once. Lettuces, leafy greens, and radishes are particularly good candidates for succession planting because there's a good chance you'll want to have a steady supply of these items. (Indeed, some lettuces are called "cut and come again" lettuces, meaning that you can first harvest some of the larger outside leaves, leaving the smaller inner leaves, and then come back and pick those after they've matured.)

You can also use succession planting with crops other than lettuce. For example, when a warm-season crop (like beans) finishes producing for the

year, you could have a different cool-season plant (like kale) that you started from seed ready to go into the garden in its place.

Finally, you can also stagger the harvest of your crops. Depending on the length of your growing season, you could plant your determinate tomato plants (i.e., those tomatoes that will ripen in a short period), cucumbers, and bush beans (many of these also provide a single flush of beans) a week or two apart so they're not all ready for the table at once. Of course, if you miscalculate or the weather has different plans and you end up with a glut of something, you can always freeze, preserve, or share it!

Good crops for succession planting include corn, cucumbers, lettuces, leafy greens (arugula, kale, collards), bush beans, peas, radishes, and carrots. Another good tip is to check the seed packet: it will often give instructions on succession planting for that particular crop. It goes without saying, of course, that another important criterion for succession planting—or indeed ANY planting—is that the crops you choose should be those that you do or would like to eat regularly. You should enjoy eating from your garden!

All in the Family: Understanding Crop Rotation

To improve your harvests, discourage disease and pests, and nourish your soil, you'll need to rotate your crops. This means you're not planting the same thing in the same spot two years in a row. But don't let yourself get stressed out by this. As horticulturist Monty Don has said, "It is rarely the end of the world if a legume follows a legume or if you grow your onions in the same place for two consecutive years. But the principle is sound and should be adhered to as far as possible." Your gardening journal or notes (see page 33) will come in handy here; try to keep at least a rough sketch of what you planted and where and when.

To better understand crop rotation, it's useful to briefly review the basics of plant divisions. You don't need to be an expert in plant taxonomy; however, you should at least know the family that any particular plant belongs to. This is easy to look up, and I've also included a chart on page 37, divided by family, for the plant profiles included in this book.

As a rule, each living being is classified by the following categories (there are subcategories, but we're keeping things simple):

Domain

Kingdom

Division

Class

Order

Family

Genus

Species

Here we're only going to concern ourselves with family, genus, and species, the latter two of which we'll discuss later. A plant family encompasses many different genera (the plural of *genus*). The Solanaceae (nightshade) family includes potatoes, eggplants, peppers, tomatillos, and goji berries; some poisonous plants, such as datura (jimsonweed), belladonna, and mandrake; as well as ornamental plants like petunias. The mint family, Lamiaceae, is home to many herbs, like basil, rosemary, thyme, oregano, and lavender, but not dill, parsley, and cilantro, which belong to the carrot family, Apiaceae. The brassica/cabbage family, Brassicaceae, includes radishes, kale, broccoli, Brussels sprouts, arugula, and many other familiar plants.

By understanding the basic plant families, you will not only boost your gardening know-how but also become a better cook, as many plants in the same family naturally taste good together. What is ratatouille other than a (mostly) Solanaceae stew!

Since plants from the same family are often susceptible to the same diseases and pests, by moving them around, you'll keep the baddies guessing. Also, some plants nourish the soil, adding nutrients (beans, which add nitrogen, are a classic example), while other plants deplete the soil, removing certain nutrients. For this reason, you'll want to rotate your plant families so that for any crop, you're not growing another member of the same plant family in that spot for a period of two to four years. For example, if you grow broccoli, a brassica, one year, you shouldn't grow cabbage, another brassica, in that same spot until several years later.

Plant Families

AMARANTHACEAE: Red-leaf amaranth (page 76); Beets (page 86); Spinach (page 154); Swiss chard (page 158)

AMARYLLIDACEAE: Chives (page 98); Garlic (page 114); Scallions (page 152)

APIACEAE: Carrots (page 96); Cilantro/coriander (page 100); Dill (page 108); Parsley (page 130)

ASTERACEAE: Lettuce (page 122)

BORAGINACEAE: Borage (page 88)

BRASSICACEAE: Arugula (page 78); Broccoli (page 90); Cabbage (page 92); Chinese cabbage (page 94); Collard greens (page 102); Kale (page 118); Radishes (page 146)

CONVOLVULACEAE: Sweet potatoes (page 156)

CUCURBITACEAE: Cucumbers (page 106); Pumpkins/winter squash (page 142); Zucchini (page 166)

FABACEAE: Beans (page 82); Edamame (page 110); Peas (page 132)

LAMIACEAE: Basil (page 80); Lavender (page 120); Mint (page 126); Oregano (page 128); Rosemary (page 148); Sage (page 150); Thyme (page 160)

POACEAE: Corn (page 104)

SOLANACEAE: Eggplant (page 112); Peppers/chiles (page 134); Potatoes (page 138); Tomatoes (page 162)

Like Peas and Carrots: Companion Planting

A final, lesser component of designing your garden plot is companion planting. This may be more than you want to think about at this stage, but it's something to keep in mind or explore later. While there isn't a lot of research on this subject, the theory behind companion planting is that certain plants grow well together and others don't. This could be because they are competing for resources (or not) or attract similar pests (or not). Good companion plants may attract pollinators or beneficial insects or produce masking smells (think: herbs) to repel and confuse pests. Other plants, such as lettuce and

radishes, can be planted among plants that are slower to mature to maximize garden yields because they'll be long gone by the time the slower crop is ready. Still other plants, like nasturtiums, may be pest magnets—a sort of sacrificial plant—that end up distracting pests from the crop you're trying to protect. Here are a few classic companion plants to try. Observe your garden over time and see what works (or doesn't work) for you.

Basil: Tomato and basil taste great together, but they're also a classic companion-planting combo. Basil is thought to repel aphids, whiteflies, and mosquitos.

Marigold and Calendula: Good for general garden pests, including beetles and root nematodes.

Nasturtium: Protects against squash bugs and attracts aphids, beetles, and caterpillars to itself so that they don't attack your crops, particularly brassicas, squash plants (cucumber, pumpkin, etc.), and tomatoes, potatoes, and peppers.

Getting Started with Seeds

Now comes the fun part!

Once you start tiptoeing your way into seeds and seed catalogs, you'll stumble across a few terms. Some of them may already be familiar to you, even if you're completely new to gardening. Still, it's worthwhile to review these terms and see what they really mean, since some are prone to common misunderstandings and others may be incompletely understood.

Let's start with **GMOs (genetically modified organisms)**, a term that may cause concern for home gardeners. You should know right away that GMO seeds are not sold to home gardeners, only to commercial farmers. In other words, you can't buy GMO seeds. Be assured that any seeds you buy in a packet are non-GMO, whether the packaging specifies that or not.

Hybrids are crosses between plant varieties. A hybrid is not at all the same thing as a GMO. Some hybrids occur naturally through pollination (see "open-pollinated," below), but many of the hybrid seeds you buy (known as F1, or first-generation seed) will have been professionally crossbred to promote certain characteristics, for example, increased yield, disease resistance, or heat/cold tolerance. Hybrids are often easier to grow because, well, they were bred for that! The downside to hybrids is that if you save the seeds produced by a hybrid plant (perhaps intending to grow new plants from them next season), they will not grow "true"—that is, the new plant will not have the same traits as the original parent plant. So if you like a particular hybrid, you will have to keep buying seeds for it every growing season.

Open-pollinated (or standard) varieties are older, inbred varieties that have been naturally pollinated. This pollination might have been by insects, birds, wind, rain, or humans. The seeds of open-pollinated plants can be saved and stored. When you plant these seeds, they will produce a plant that is very similar to the parent plant from which you obtained the seed. Open-pollinated options often boast better flavor and more intriguing varieties, but they don't necessarily have the same beneficial traits (like disease resistance, yield, and so on) as hybrids.

While the term has some cachet and may be associated with quality, **heirlooms** are simply open-pollinated varieties that are at least fifty years old—and often much older. As with open-pollinated varieties, they have a greater diversity and can be more flavorful than hybrids, but they also share the same downsides.

Treated seeds have been coated with a pesticide/insecticide and are often dyed bright colors. It's thought that treated seeds might negatively affect bees and other pollinators. Organic farmers are not permitted to use treated seed for their crops (they will not be classified as "organic"), so if you're planning on gardening organically, treated seeds should be avoided.

What Should Your Garden Grow?

Hopefully you have a much better idea of what you want to plant than when you started reading this book, but let's focus on a few general criteria.

Grow plants you like and want to eat. Think about the fruits, vegetables, and herbs that you already tend to eat and that often grace your plate. If you think—as I do—that Swiss chard and beets taste like dirt, no matter how beautiful they are to look at, then you won't eat them, so there's no reason they should take up precious space in your garden plot. We all have our individual preferences (and, in some cases, dietary restrictions), so plan accordingly. If you love green beans, potatoes, corn, parsley, and basil, then choose appealing varieties of those to grow. Focus on staples you know your family will eat and enjoy. Relatedly, if you like to have some of a particular crop but don't love having it all the time, maybe stick with one or two plants; there's no need to take up a whole row with arugula if you eat it only a few times a year.

Start small (and slow). As I mentioned earlier (page 30), it can be hard to resist the sheer abundance that seed catalogs offer. Beyond that, you might also be incredibly enthusiastic about getting started. That's understandable, but try to channel that excitement into smart planning and editing of your garden. More is not always better, because you can get overwhelmed if you go too big too quickly. Sketch out on paper where you plan to put everything so you're sure it will fit; that will help you keep your garden manageable.

Be picky about what you grow. We've covered some of this before, but you'll have greater success if you select crops that tend to grow well where you live. Determine the length of your growing season (see page 6), and/or if you're in the US, determine your growing zone (check the USDA Plant Hardiness Zone Map at https://planthardiness .ars.usda.gov). When you select seeds, read the back of the packet for valuable information on the seeds' optimal growing conditions. (You can also find this information online or in the seed catalog.) Usually, the packet will offer excellent details on the ideal temperature for the crop, its frost hardiness (meaning whether it will survive a frost), and the number of days to harvest (this is why it's key to know the length of your growing season). Don't forget that you can also ask more experienced fellow local gardeners what grows well for them. This is a great way to learn other people's tips and tricks, as well as what works and what doesn't in your area. Local knowledge could very well save you years of trial and error. It's also a wonderful way to meet and socialize with like-minded people around a safe and positive hobby!

Do keep in mind, however, that everyone's growing conditions (soil, light, and so on) will be a little bit different, so not all advice will apply perfectly to your own situation.

Choose your cool- and warm-season crops. Based on your garden plan, choose a range of crops that will mature throughout the growing season, starting with cool-season plants.

Starting Seeds Indoors

Let's start off with a question that might be at the top of your mind as a beginner: Is it necessary to grow your veggies and herbs from seed? Absolutely not. Follow-up question: Should you give it a try? Definitely.

Of course, you can always purchase nursery transplants that are ready to go out into the garden; however, if you start from seed, you'll have access to a much larger variety of plants—literally anything you can order from a seed company, versus just the varieties your local nursery decides to grow or carry. Starting from seed is cheaper than buying an established plant, and you can also get a head start on the growing season.

But the main reason to grow from seed is this: it's fun. No matter how new or experienced you are, there's nothing quite like watching a plant grow from a tiny seed into a full-size plant. It never gets old. Just that one seed contains all the genetic material needed to produce a massive, vining cucumber plant, or a tall stalk of corn, or a tomato plant laden with fruit. From so little comes so much; it's amazing. So even if you just pop a few basil or green bean seeds into a pot, I urge you to give it a try.

That said, if you're starting your garden late in the year or you just want to simplify your life, there's no shame in buying transplants, so don't let the idea of growing from seed be a barrier to getting started on your garden. You may also buy transplants selectively: for example, something catches your eye, you realize you forgot to start a crop you want to grow, the seeds you started didn't work out for one reason or another (e.g., poor germination, damping-off; see page 50).

Some seeds are best started indoors, while others can be sown directly in the garden (called direct sowing or direct seeding). The seed packet will indicate whether a seed should be started indoors, sown directly, or if it doesn't matter either way.

You'll need a few simple items to get started:

Sterile seed-starting mix: You can make your own seed-starting mix, but it's also readily available at nurseries, garden centers, and big-box retailers. Do not use garden soil, which may have fungi, microbes, weed seeds, insect eggs, and other things that might kill or set back your seedlings. Plus, it's too dense, while seed-starting mix is light. For sustainability and to reduce your carbon footprint, look for a peat-free mixture. Usually, coconut coir will be used to replace the peat moss.

Small containers to plant your seeds: You can go as DIY or as fancy as you want here. You can buy seed-starting trays (sometimes called germination trays) with a dome cover. These can have six, twelve, or more cells. You can also be creative and reuse plastic yogurt containers (add a hole in the bottom for drainage), takeout containers (again, add drainage), cardboard egg cartons, or even toilet paper rolls (which you can line up in a container, fill with soil, and then later plant the seedlings, roll and all, directly in the garden). Just make sure whatever you use is small, no more than a few inches deep, and has good drainage. If you're reusing materials from previous years, be sure to sterilize them to avoid passing along pests or diseases to this year's seedlings.

Grow lights: You might think of grow lights as more than you want to deal with—if that's the case, skip them. You can put your seedlings by a very sunny window and rotate them for even growth. However, window light is often not strong or bright enough, particularly at the time of year when you'll be starting seeds. Grow lights are now quite affordable, with both fluorescent and LED options available, and they'll really help your seedlings start life as strong as possible. I have had good success with adjustable-height LED grow light panels, which you can raise as your seedlings get taller. These integrated systems are good for beginners because you can put them anywhere; you don't have to find somewhere to suspend 4-foot (1.2 m) shop lights (if you're like me, any time there's an instruction to hang something, it automatically seems like too much of a challenge), and you don't have to worry (too much) about the complexities of lumens and degrees Kelvin. The downside is that the panel size is limited, as is the maximum height you can raise the panel. And you'll pay a little bit more for the convenience. If you have wire shelving units, though, it's really easy to attach grow lights to them (even *I* can manage this), and you can choose whichever ones work best for you. If you opt for grow lights, I also recommend getting an outlet timer, so you don't have to worry about switching the lights on and off. I use one that I can program with my smartphone to operate for 16 hours on and 8 hours off each day until the seedlings are well established. If you're interested in learning more about grow lights, check out Leslie Halleck's wonderful book *Gardening Under Lights*.

Heat mat: Some seeds require warmth to germinate, so you can help them along by placing your containers on a heat mat. This is more of an optional item, even though it's relatively inexpensive, as you may have warm places in your home that would work just as well.

Planting, Step-by-Step

Follow these nine easy steps to start growing from seed. You won't be starting all your seeds at once; instead, count back from when you want to put them in the garden to decide when to start which crops. The seed packets will tell you when to start them based on the last frost date for your area.

1. Gather your supplies. Round up your seeds, seed-starting mix, and containers.
2. Moisten your seed-starting mix. Seed-starting mix tends to be quite dry, so it can be helpful to moisten it by adding some water before starting. This also helps the seeds stay in place instead of floating around the top of the container once you've sown them.
3. Fill the containers. Add enough seed-starting mix to fill your containers to ¼ to ½ inch (6 to 13 mm) from the top. The mix should be pressed in firmly but not packed in.
4. Plant the seeds. Following the instructions on the packet for depth, sow your seeds as thinly as possible—just a few per container if the seeds are very small and one per container for large seeds. Press down

gently. Sift some more seed-starting mix over the seeds to cover. Keep in mind that not every seed will germinate, and some seedlings will be stronger than others.

5. **Label the containers.** You can use whatever you have on hand—plant tags, wooden craft sticks, masking tape, etc.

6. **Water the seeds.** You have a few options for watering the seeds. You can gently water them with a spray bottle, being careful not to disturb them too much, or, if the seed-starting mix is still a bit dry, you can put the containers in a larger tray and add some water into the bottom tray. The soil will absorb the water through the drainage holes. Start with a small amount of water and wait until it's absorbed. If the medium is still dry, you can add a bit more until it's evenly moistened.

7. **Cover.** If you're using germination trays, cover with the dome. Otherwise, cover the containers with plastic wrap or a plastic bag to maintain humidity.

8. **Place the tray in a warm, well-lighted place.** While many seeds don't need light to germinate, if you start them in good light right away, the light will be right there waiting for them the second they pop their heads above the soil. This also helps you avoid leggy plants (when the plant grows tall and spindly), which are weak, more prone to pests and disease, and likely to struggle in outdoor conditions.

9. **Check for germination, water needs, and light.** As soon as the seedlings germinate, remove the covering and place them under your grow light (if they aren't there already) for 16 hours a day, followed by 8 hours of darkness. If you're not using a grow light, make sure they're in the sunniest spot available and rotate the tray a quarter turn every few days to promote even growth. The covering should keep the humidity in, particularly for a few days, but if you notice that the soil is starting to dry out, then water them from the bottom as in step 6. Make sure you adjust the space between the plants and the grow light as the seedlings get taller to avoid scorching their tender leaves. After about 2 weeks, you can reduce the grow light cycle to 12 to 14 hours of light per day.

Understanding Seed Packets

Seed packets provide a wealth of valuable information in a very condensed format. Let's break it down.

Culture/planting instructions: "Culture" refers to the process of cultivating plants. And on the packet, it's where you'll learn when and how you should plant your seeds. For example, you might see something like "Start seeds indoors 4 to 6 weeks before transplanting to the garden" or "Transplant to the garden after the last frost." The soil temperature lags behind the outdoor temperature by a couple of weeks, so you can use that to calculate when to start a particular seed. You might also see an instruction like "Sow directly when the danger of frost has passed and the soil is warm." Or you might be given directions for both starting the seeds indoors and direct sowing. The instructions might also specify compost needs, fertilizer requirements, ideal soil types (e.g., well drained), and/or soil temperatures. Culture requirements are yet another reason to start small at the beginning. You'll be getting the hang of caring for plants with (often) very different needs, and if you go overboard, it might start to feel like a bit of a juggling act.

Harvest: This information is usually given in number of days to harvest. For anything you start from seed, this generally means the number of days from when you transplant the seedling to the garden. It might also indicate how you know the plants are ready for harvest (for example, what length of cucumber or bean is harvest-ready) and whether continued picking will encourage the plant to produce more.

Germination: Different seeds germinate at different rates, and the seed packet usually indicates how long germination takes. Germination also depends on soil temperatures. Some crops germinate in just a few days, while others may take several weeks, so be patient.

Plant height: This indicates how tall the mature plant will be.

Spacing: This tells you how much space to put between each plant and between each row of plants.

Sowing depth: This might say something like "surface," or give a more exact depth, such as ¼ inch (.5 cm), ½ inch (1.3 cm), 1 inch (2.5 cm), and so on.

Diseases and pests: Occasionally, the packet will indicate the diseases and pests this particular variety is susceptible to and how to prevent and/or manage them.

Light: Many crops need full sun, but some crops do well in partial shade.

Other: The packet might indicate the germination rate (what percentage of the seeds can be expected to germinate) and how many seeds are in the packet.

When watering your seedlings, do so ideally from the bottom, but don't let them sit in water. Keep them consistently moist but not waterlogged (which could lead to root rot). After a week or two, you can also start giving them a very weak, balanced fertilizer to help support strong growth. But—and this is important—the fertilizer must really be diluted (for example, if the label recommends 1 tablespoon per gallon of water, you can start with 1 teaspoon per gallon, depending on the strength of the fertilizer), as too much fertilizer could kill your tender seedlings and/or burn their roots. A balanced fertilizer is one where the proportions of nitrogen, phosphorus, and potassium (NPK) are equal (this will be listed on the label—for example, "5-5-5"). If you happen to grow houseplants and this is your first foray into edible gardening, you'll notice that many edible plants need more fertilizer than what you're used to.

Troubleshooting

By watering from the bottom, you not only avoid disrupting the root systems and growth of these tiny plants but also help prevent a problem common to seed starting: damping-off.

Damping-off is a fungal disease that eventually causes the seedlings to collapse and die. To help prevent damping-off, ensure that your seedlings have proper air circulation, water from the bottom, and make sure that you don't overwater.

Another common issue you may run into is insufficient light. If you're not giving your seedlings enough light, they'll become long, stringy, spindly, and weak ("leggy"), rather than compact and full. To combat this, move your seedlings to a sunnier location or put them under a grow light.

Kill Your Darlings: Thinning

As the seedlings grow, you need to remove the weaker plants. This process is called thinning, and it can feel like a painful task because you don't want to kill these brand-new baby plants. However, thinning ensures that each plant you keep will have the best opportunity to grow big and strong (and not be crowded out by other plants). It also means that you won't end up with an inordinate number of the same type of plant. Just because twenty basil seeds sprouted doesn't mean you want twenty basil plants, believe me! If you're thinning herbs or greens, you can just toss the thinned leaves into a salad. Otherwise, just pinch or clip the seedling you'd like to thin at the root level. Don't pull it out like a weed or you may damage the root systems of the other plants.

When should you thin your seedlings? The answer will vary depending on the plant, but in all cases it should be, at minimum, when the seedlings have grown one or two sets of true leaves. This will allow you to better assess the strength of the individual plant. (The first pair of leaves that emerges from your seed is known as the cotyledon. If you happen to take a close look, you might notice that these first leaves don't look like a basil leaf, or a tomato leaf, or a bean leaf, or a leaf of whatever it is you planted. The plant's second set of leaves will be true leaves.)

A weak plant might be floppy, have malformed leaves, or exhibit other obvious signs that it's not as strong as other candidates. Now, if none of them look particularly weak—they all look pretty much the same—then just choose whichever seems to be the strongest. In the end, you should have just one plant per container.

Moving on Up: Transplanting Seedlings Indoors

Particularly if you've used small containers to start your seeds, you may find that the seedlings outgrow their containers and need to be moved to a larger pot before they're quite ready to go out to the garden. One way to assess whether that's the case is to have a look at the root system. Gently place your hand over the top of the container with the stem of the plant in the V between your index finger and middle finger. Turn the container over and carefully lift it away from the soil. If you notice lots of visible roots wrapped around the soil, it's time to transplant the seedling to a bigger pot.

Your Garden Tool Kit

Just as you would stock a kitchen with the right implements, so too should you plan on having a few key pieces of quality equipment on hand to make your gardening experience easier and more efficient. In keeping with my philosophy of taking the path of least resistance, I've kept this list as minimal as possible, but as with any endeavor, you can always start with a few tools and then add more as you find you need them. To keep costs down, you may be able to borrow some of these items from friends, family, or neighbors, or find them at secondhand stores. I provide more specific equipment for starting seeds on page 45.

Shovel and spade: There is a difference between these tools! A shovel has a rounded tip. Use it for scooping things, such as adding and moving soil when you incorporate compost. A spade has a straight front edge, which is designed for digging and making edgings.

Hoe: A garden hoe can be used for weeding, cultivating the soil, and making rows for direct sowing seeds. It can also be used to clear areas of leaves and other debris. The most common garden hoe has a flat, bladelike head, but there are many different variations available.

Garden (spading) fork: A garden fork generally has four tines and is ideal for aerating the soil and breaking up clumps. Make sure the tines are sturdy. You're not going for *American Gothic* pitchfork vibes here; you need something that you can actually dig into the ground with.

Rake: A garden rake is used for smoothing the soil into a fine, even layer to make it ready for planting. Again, make sure to choose a sturdy one with metal tines, not the lightweight kind used to rake fall leaves.

Trowel: A trowel is a small handheld shovel. You'll use it to dig small holes when transplanting seedlings to the garden, but it has numerous other uses, including weeding.

Pruning shears: Shears are useful for harvesting crops and cutting back plants.

Gardening scissors or pocketknife: For smaller harvesting or maintenance jobs, you may prefer to use scissors or a simple pocketknife. Sometimes called garden snips, gardening scissors are great for herbs and green beans.

Hose: A garden hose will be invaluable for manually irrigating your garden. Make sure both the hose and all its fittings are nontoxic and suitable to be used on edible crops.

Watering can: A watering can is great for watering plants once they've been transplanted and for fertilizing. Try to find one that has a removable rose (sprinkler) attachment for watering jobs that require a gentler touch, such as seedlings or direct sowing.

Wheelbarrow: You'll need a way to transport compost, soil, and other heavy objects around the garden. While a wheelbarrow can be a bit of an investment, it will make your life much easier. You can also use it to haul garden debris, like end-of-season plants, to the compost pile.

Bucket or basket: You'll need somewhere to put your delicious harvest. Chances are that you already have something on hand that will serve this purpose.

Kneeling pad: Because you'll be spending a lot of time on your knees, an inexpensive knee-pad can be just the thing to make that time more comfortable. Another option is a folding garden stool.

Gloves: Gloves protect your hands from thorns and other sharp or rough surfaces. They also inhibit blisters and keep your hands clean, especially under the nails! Use dedicated gloves specifically designed for gardening.

Wooden board: A wooden board (a few feet long) is convenient for making a straight drill (furrow) for directly sowing seeds in a row. You can even mark it off with common measurements for spacing seeds and plants.

Other personal items to include are a **wide-brimmed sun hat**, which both protects you from the sun and helps keep the bugs away; **garden clogs or waterproof boots**; and **broad-spectrum sunscreen** (a must!).

Garden Maintenance

The plants are in the ground. The seeds are planted. Now we turn our attention to how we'll keep our plants healthy and growing well, always keeping in mind that we control only part of the process. Mother Nature is really the one in charge.

Watering

Watering correctly is essential. By paying attention to what makes soil healthy, such as incorporating organic material and mulching, you can help reduce your watering needs. Mulch (see page 21) in particular reduces evaporation and keeps the soil cooler. But you will also need a watering strategy. Inconsistent watering—whether underwatering or overwatering—can stress plants, making them more prone to pests and diseases.

Generally, it's better to soak your plants deeply and less frequently than to water them shallowly and often. You want the soil well below the surface to stay moist. This will also encourage the roots to grow down, rather than stay near the surface where they'll dry out more quickly.

Water is (obviously) heavy, so make your job as easy as possible. If you have only a very small garden, a **watering can** might be an option for you, particularly if you have a rain catchment system near your garden or if you're growing in containers. The most convenient but also most expensive watering option is to use **soaker hoses and drip irrigation**. These dribble moisture into the soil, allowing it to penetrate down deep over a set period of time. Many gardeners simply like to use **regular hoses** for watering, not only because it's easy but also because they can use the watering session as a way of keeping an eye on the plants. Here are some simple tips on watering technique:

1. **When you water, water the soil, not the plant itself.** The water needs to go into the soil—where it can irrigate the plant. Avoid splashing water onto the leaves, which can lead to problems such as fungal infections.

2. **Adjust your watering schedule to your garden's needs.**
   It's difficult to provide general guidance on how often to water your garden, since this will vary depending on your climate, the amount of rainfall you typically get, the time of year, and so on. It's fair to say, though, that you'll be watering more often during the hot days of summer.

3. **To determine whether your garden needs water, feel the soil.**
   With your hand or a trowel, dig down into the soil several inches, below the mulch layer. Is it cool and moist? If so, you can hold off. If it's dry, it's time to get out the hose.

4. **Water deeply.** It may take some time to get the hang of this. After you water, you may want to wait a little and then feel the soil again to see if it's damp a few inches down.

5. **Water early.** To reduce evaporation, it's better to give your plants a soaking early in the day, before the sun heats things up. Try to avoid watering the garden when the sun is at its peak; water will be lost due to evaporation from the soil's surface. You can also water in the early evening, but there is an increased risk of fungal issues if water remains on the leaves overnight.

6. **Get a rain gauge.** A rain gauge can help you determine how much water your garden receives from rainfall and whether you can skip watering by hand.

7. **Don't be tricked by wilt.** While wilt can be an indicator that your plants need water, it's also common for some plants to wilt in the hottest part of the day. Wait to see if they perk up later in the day, and feel the soil (see tip 3) to see whether watering is really needed.

8. **Watch the containers.** Plants in containers will need much more water than those in the ground or in a raised bed, especially depending on the weather and the stage of the growth cycle. Some water-loving plants like tomatoes and cucumbers may require watering more than once a day in hot weather.

Fertilizers

The most important fertilizer for your plant is healthy soil that has been enriched with organic matter. No fertilizer you add can substitute for that. However, as your plants use up the nutrients in the soil, adding fertilizers will often be necessary, particularly for fruiting crops such as cucumber and tomato.

In general, fertilizers supply three key nutrients that plants need: nitrogen (N), phosphorus (P), and potassium (K, also known as potash). Roughly speaking, nitrogen supports green leafy growth, phosphorus promotes root health, and potassium supports flowering and fruiting. Plants also require calcium, sulfur, and magnesium, as well as trace amounts of other elements. A soil test can help you determine whether your soil has any deficiencies in these areas. Fertilizers may be organic or nonorganic and water-insoluble or water-soluble.

Organic fertilizers include well-rotted manure, bloodmeal and bonemeal, fish emulsion, and seaweed fertilizer, among others. Organic fertilizers greatly support soil health but work slowly, so it requires a bit more planning to get them into the soil with enough time to nourish your plants.

Nonorganic fertilizers are created in a lab and manufactured commercially. They're widely available in nurseries and big-box stores. They work quickly but do not improve soil health and, if overused, can even be detrimental to the soil as well as to your plants.

Granular fertilizers, sometimes called slow-release fertilizers, are initially water-insoluble and need to be mixed into the soil. Over time, the soil microbes and water will break these fertilizers down.

Water-soluble fertilizers are easily dissolved in water, so they work quickly. They come in both organic and nonorganic options. Organic examples include fish emulsion and kelp fertilizer, and nonorganic options include any sort of commercially available fertilizer crystals that you dissolve in water.

Containers 101

Got garden envy? If you only have a balcony, or even if you have no outdoor space at all, you can still do some gardening. Those limitations, in fact, can sometimes inspire incredible creativity. If you are facing such limitations, many of the tips in this book will still apply; you'll just need to tweak them slightly.

If You've Got a Balcony or Patio

If you're lucky enough to have a *bit* of outdoor space, such as a balcony or patio, a good option is to grow plants in containers. You'll still need to ensure they get enough light (at least 6 hours of full sun per day), and you'll want to be even pickier about what you grow. Is it most useful to have an herb garden that you can count on throughout the season? Would you instead prefer a regular supply of lettuce? Or do you have your heart set on growing tomatoes? You'll be amazed at how much produce you can fit into a small space! But first, make sure it's permitted in your building, and also that your balcony can withstand the extra weight of the soil-filled containers.

SOIL

For containers, look for a basic potting mix and enrich it with compost or worm castings, both of which are commercially available.

CONTAINERS

The size of your containers will depend on the kind of crops you want to grow. Lettuce can be grown in long, shallow, window box–like planters. Herbs can be grown in pots. Tomatoes often need a container with a capacity of at least 5 gallons (18 L), but larger is optimal. As for the material the container is made of, there are many good options. You can go with terra cotta or plastic, or even use grow bags; just keep in mind that terra cotta is porous and dries out more quickly than plastic containers, which means more watering. Personally, I like elevated self-watering planters that are the perfect height for easy plant care.

THINK UP

Vertical gardening, using trellises and other supports, can help you expand your available space.

WATERING

With container gardening, you'll need to stay on top of your watering more than you do with in-ground gardening. As mentioned, in the hottest part of the summer, some crops may need to be watered more than once a day. But don't fall into the trap of overwatering either. Feel the soil (about 1 to 2 inches, or 2.5 to 5 cm, down) to make sure the plant needs it. Also remember that not every plant will need water at the same time.

FERTILIZING

Container plants exhaust the key nutrients in the soil (NPK; see page 59) faster than garden-grown plants, so you'll need a more regular and consistent fertilizing regime. It's a good practice to mix some organic granular fertilizer into your potting mix and then use a water-soluble fertilizer periodically as part of your regular watering.

Some plants, like herbs and peppers, are ideally suited to containers simply because they don't get too big. Other plants come in varieties that are especially suited for container gardening. For instance, beans, cucumbers, peppers, and tomatoes all come in compact, bush, dwarf, and determinate varieties that are perfect for growing in containers. Container-specific varieties are often indicated as such in seed catalogs and on websites.

If You've Got No Outdoor Space at All

But what if you have no outdoor space at all, not even a window box? If that's your situation, you still have the option of gardening entirely indoors. High-tech hydroponic countertop gardens (which became incredibly popular at the beginning of the COVID-19 pandemic in 2020) make it easy to grow herbs, lettuce, tomatoes, peppers, and even strawberries in the comfort of your own home. These all-in-one units come with LED lights, Wi-Fi, and smartphone controls, and they'll even tell you when it's time to water or

fertilize your plants. This is no doubt a pricier option, but it can be a great way for beginners, particularly busy professionals, to experience the freshness of homegrown food. Countertop gardens also allow you to grow year-round. How would you like fresh cherry tomatoes and basil in February? If you're a little more experienced and prefer a more DIY route, you can grow food indoors using your own setup with grow lights.

Pests and Diseases

The best defense against pests and diseases in the garden is a healthy ecosystem. Both pests and diseases are more likely to proliferate on plants that are stressed. By tending to the health of the soil and ensuring that your plants receive the proper care (which means taking the time to learn about their needs), as well as by simply keeping an eye on them daily, you'll help forestall many problems before they have a chance to start. It's all about practicing good garden hygiene. Here are some basic tips for preventing and managing pests.

Monitor water needs. Both lack of water and overwatering can stress a plant, making it more prone to pests and disease. Ensure that your plants receive adequate water, and water the soil, not the leaves, to prevent fungal infections.

Mulch well. A thick layer of mulch will help retain moisture in the soil and suppress weeds, but you'll still need to . . .

Weed regularly. If you're vigilant and regularly remove weeds, you'll ensure that your plants aren't competing with weeds for essential soil nutrients. But keep in mind that some plants have shallow root systems, so weed carefully to avoid disturbing them.

Prune and remove plants as needed. It's much easier to quickly remove diseased leaves or even a whole diseased plant than to deal with issues that have spread throughout multiple plants in the garden.

Grow flowering plants. Many flowering plants attract pollinators and beneficial insects to the garden. Calendula, marigold, yarrow, dill, violas, borage, nasturtium, and sweet pea are just a few additions that will not only make your garden more beautiful but will also let nature do the pest-prevention work for you. Beneficial insects include lacewings, assassin bugs, ladybugs, hoverflies, and others. Always make sure you know what the good bugs look like before you kill insects you find in the garden. You can also buy beneficial nematodes, which are microscopic organisms that you add to the soil to help manage insect pests. Toads, birds, and bats eat insect pests as well.

Use floating row covers. These thin, gauzy fabric covers, usually made of polypropylene, let light and air pass through but protect plants from insect attacks.

Plant the right plant at the right time. If the soil temperature is too cold or the daytime temperatures are too hot, certain plants won't thrive, making them more susceptible to pests and disease. Transplant or direct-sow seeds when conditions are right for your location, remembering that some plants are cool-season crops while others are warm-season crops.

Space your plants. Plants need airflow. Placing plants too close together makes them more likely to have pest problems, not to mention that their growth may be stunted.

Consider a fence. If larger critters, such as rabbits, groundhogs, or deer, regularly come to check out what your garden has to offer, installing a fence can help you keep your precious crops to yourself.

Pick your pests. Many pests, such as Japanese beetles, squash bugs, and Colorado potato beetles, can be removed by hand.

Practice crop rotation. See "All in the Family" on page 35.

PLANT DISEASES

When it comes to plant diseases, prevention through good garden hygiene is the best medicine. In addition to the tips mentioned in the previous section, choosing disease-resistant varieties can help. While many pest infestations can be controlled or managed, plant diseases can spread fast, and the best solution is often to remove and destroy the affected leaves or entire plants before they are able to infect others in the garden. Diseased plants should not be composted.

Blights. Early blight and late blight are fungal diseases that can devastate crops, particularly tomatoes and potatoes. Early blight occurs with warm, humid weather. It produces brown spots on leaves, often in concentric circles and starting toward the base of the plant. It can also affect the fruit. Affected plants should be destroyed. To prevent early blight in tomatoes, choose varieties that indicate blight resistance, practice crop rotation, ensure adequate airflow around the plants, and avoid splashing the leaves when watering. You can also remove the bottom leaves of the tomato plant as it grows. Organic fungicides can be used to combat early blight; they're often only effective when used early.

Late blight occurs in cooler temperatures than early blight. It produces dark, watery-looking lesions on the leaves and stems of the plant, as well as rot in the fruit or tuber (late blight, in fact, was the cause of the Irish Potato Famine in the 1840s). Affected plants should be destroyed. Choose varieties that are resistant to late blight and practice crop rotation. Affected fruits or tubers should not be eaten.

Powdery mildew. Very common on cucumbers and other members of the gourd family, powdery mildew is a fungal infection that looks exactly like what its name indicates: a white, powdery substance that covers the tops of the leaves. Affected leaves should be removed. A solution of baking soda, dish soap, and water (1 tablespoon baking soda and 1 teaspoon dish soap in 1 gallon of water) sprayed on the leaves often helps, but test it out on a single leaf first to ensure your plant can tolerate it. Increasing air circulation around plants is also helpful.

Mosaic viruses. This group of viruses affects many different kinds of plants, particularly tomatoes, cucumbers, peppers, and squash. The foliage will look mottled and may become twisted and deformed. These viruses are typically spread by insect pests, so choosing resistant varieties can help, as can using floating row covers. These viruses are also sometimes spread by garden tools that have not been properly cleaned (or at all), or simply by handling affected plants and then healthy ones. There is no cure for mosaic viruses, so affected plants should be destroyed.

Root rot. Root rot can happen when the soil is too moist, often due to overwatering. This excess moisture creates the perfect conditions for fungi to proliferate, which will then lead to wilting and yellowing, and eventually the death of the plant. Ensure that your soil is well drained and that you don't overwater, and remove affected plants. See page 56 for tips on when and how to water.

COMMON INSECT PESTS

We don't have the space to cover every kind of insect that may appear in your garden, but you can find identification guides online to help you determine which are beneficial and which are not. Here are some of the most common garden insect pests you're likely to come across. You may have others specific to where you live—check with fellow gardeners to see what the most common pests affecting their crops are.

Note: If you decide to use neem oil or *Bacillus thuringiensis* (Bt), follow the manufacturer's instructions, as multiple treatments are usually required. Both work when used preventively as well. For more information, see page 72.

Aphids. These tiny insects come in a range of colors, including red, pink, and green, and they like nothing more than to eat new plant growth. They can be controlled with sharp sprays of water on the affected

areas (typically the undersides of leaves). Spraying neem oil can help, and sticky traps can also reduce their numbers. They are a tasty treat to certain beneficial insects. See page 64 for more information about attracting these insects to your garden.

Cabbage looper caterpillars and cabbage worms. Brassicas are commonly affected by these two pests, which will eat holes in leaves and also burrow into the head of cabbage or broccoli or cauliflower. If you see small white butterflies fluttering around your garden, it's not a good sign. These little butterflies may seem cute, but they are very likely laying eggs on your cabbage crops— check under the leaves! A good way to prevent cabbage looper caterpillars and cabbage worms is to install floating row covers. If these pests have already arrived in your garden, beneficial insects and birds will help manage them, as will picking off the eggs and caterpillars/worms by hand and using sticky traps. Bt will kill them, as will food-grade diatomaceous earth.

Colorado potato beetles. These striped beetles are big fans of nightshade family crops, particularly potatoes, tomatoes, peppers, and eggplant. Like other pests, they lay their eggs on the undersides of leaves. Potato beetle eggs are particularly noticeable because they are yellow orange. As with other insect pests, checking your plants regularly is important. Beneficial insects are great allies for controlling these pests; you can also try Bt. Remove beetles and crush eggs by hand.

Cucumber beetles. There are two different genera of cucumber beetles; one is striped and the other is spotted. Unfortunately, they not only feed on plants but also spread cucumber mosaic virus and bacterial wilt. Again, you can pick off the beetles, eggs, and larvae by hand, or try neem oil, diatomaceous earth, or Bt.

Flea beetles. These small, jumping beetles are common on many types of vegetable crops. They cause leaf damage by creating small holes and are at their most troublesome in the spring when they first emerge for the year. Damage can be prevented by planting crops a bit later, ensuring the seedlings are strong and stable, and using floating row covers. Beneficial insects, including nematodes, will help control their numbers.

Japanese beetles. Iridescent green and copper in color, Japanese beetles might look attractive, but they can be a real problem for many kinds of vegetation. Like many other insect pests, they consume your plants' leaves, so look out for the beetles themselves to confirm the source of the problem. You can remove them by hand and drown them in soapy water, or spray your plants with neem oil. Diatomaceous earth applied regularly can also help, as will beneficial nematodes. Admittedly, though, Japanese beetles are quite a challenge.

Leaf miners. Leaf miners bore through leaves, creating wavy patterns of lines. To keep the problem under control, remove the affected leaves and keep the area weed-free. Beneficial insects are also helpful. As a preventive measure, use floating row covers.

Mexican bean beetles. Don't be fooled by the appearance of this destructive beetle. Superficially, it looks very much like a ladybug (a beneficial insect you want to attract to your garden). However, the Mexican bean beetle is more bronze, orange, or copper in color. These beetles, particularly during their larval stage, are capable of decimating your bean crop. They will defoliate the bean plants, leaving behind a lacy pattern on the leaves. Look for them on the underside of the leaves; they can also feed on the beans themselves. Floating row covers can be used to preventively protect crops. You can pick off the beetles by hand and crush the eggs and larvae. Spray your plants with neem. For heavy infestations, you may need to destroy the plants.

Slugs and snails. These mollusks love cool, damp conditions and prefer to dine at night or on cloudy days. To eliminate these critters, just head out to your garden at night and catch them in the act! Pick them from your plants by hand, or sink a plastic container filled with beer into the soil—they'll climb right into it and drown. If nighttime slug hunting isn't for you,

food-grade diatomaceous earth will help. You can also try laying out wooden boards on the soil, as slugs and snails will hide underneath them; in the morning, simply lift the board and collect them. Also look for them in their favorite hiding places, such as under stones, in garden debris, and in other moist, dark places.

Squash bugs. Large and flat, squash bugs are attracted to members of the gourd family (Cucurbitaceae), including pumpkin, squash, cucumber, and melon. They feed on and damage the foliage of these plants, weakening the plants and affecting their ability to take in water and nutrients. The bugs will lay eggs on the undersides of leaves and on stems; these visible eggs can simply be crushed. As with slugs and snails, wooden boards left near the affected plants can help attract the bugs, which will then be in a convenient location to be collected in the morning. Good plant hygiene is also very important. After harvesting your squash in late fall, make sure to remove the plants completely—otherwise, you're just providing these bugs with a comfy overwintering shelter!

Tomato hornworms. An intriguing-looking green-and-white caterpillar, the tomato hornworm feasts on the leaves of—you guessed it—tomatoes, as well as other nightshade family members, such as eggplant, peppers, and potatoes. This large caterpillar (up to

4 inches, or 10 cm, long) can appear camouflaged because of its color. The adults turn into large, 4- to 5-inch (10 to 13 cm) moths. Individual hornworms can be removed by hand. Beneficial insects can also help, particularly the paper wasp, which is parasitic. The wasp lays eggs on the back of the hornworm, and as the eggs hatch and the wasps emerge, they kill the worm. While hornworms can be mostly controlled by hand, for a more widespread infestation, you can try Bt.

Whiteflies. Primarily affecting tomatoes, beans, peppers, and cucumbers, whiteflies are small insects that gather on the underside of leaves. Whiteflies are as annoying as they are common—it's almost guaranteed that you'll have to contend with them at some point in your gardening journey. These beasties are troublesome because in addition to feeding on the plant's juices, they secrete honeydew, a sticky substance that can lead to sooty mold, a fungal infection. The good thing is, whiteflies are easy to spot because of their color and behavior—if you shake an affected branch, they'll fly off in a cloud. They're especially common in warmer climates and may arrive later in the summer in more northerly latitudes. Like aphids, you can spray whiteflies with sharp streams of water, but you'll also need to remove the affected leaves. Sticky traps can help reduce their numbers, as can beneficial insects. Neem oil may help.

ORGANIC PEST CONTROLS

Ideally, you should be able to deal with garden pests mainly (if perhaps not exclusively) through proper garden hygiene, common-sense prevention, the aid of beneficial insects, and other manual and natural measures. The following solutions are organic and effective but they are certainly not without their downsides. If you decide to use one of these options, always use it carefully and follow the manufacturer's instructions to the letter. Test a small part of the plant before spraying more widely.

Bacillus thuringiensis (Bt) is a biological form of pest control that is permitted in organic gardening. Bt is a bacterium that lives in soil; it produces proteins that are toxic to the larvae of a plethora of insect pests when consumed. Thankfully, Bt is not toxic to humans. Since the bacteria must be consumed by the pest's larvae in order to work, regular reapplication of Bt is necessary. It should be noted that Bt is safe for honeybees, birds, and beneficial insects. However, since it is toxic to many caterpillars, it can harm the larvae of butterflies.

Neem oil is a naturally occurring pesticide extracted from the seeds of the neem tree, which is native to the Indian subcontinent and was subsequently introduced in many other parts of the world. Neem oil is commonly used in dandruff shampoos and skincare products, and has a long history of use in Ayurvedic medicine. The active compound in neem oil, azadirachtin, disrupts the development of larvae and suppresses the appetite of many insect pests, including aphids, whiteflies, mites, and other soft-bodied insects. It also works well as a fungicide. Look for 100 percent cold-pressed neem oil and dilute it according to the manufacturer's instructions, which will typically include adding a small amount of mild dish soap. For maximum effect, neem oil should be applied in early morning or evening only, and never in direct sunlight, because it is UV sensitive. Reapplying will often be necessary. It should be noted that neem oil can affect beneficial insects, too, so you should use it carefully and in a targeted fashion.

Food-grade diatomaceous earth (DE) is a powder made of the fossilized remains of diatoms, a kind of algae. When insect pests, including slugs, snails, beetles, and caterpillars, travel across a surface dusted with DE, the abrasive powder physically cuts up their bodies, leading to dehydration and death. DE can be sprinkled in a circle around plants that you'd like to protect. It can also be dusted on leaves, but don't do it when the plant is flowering because it can harm pollinators. Note that DE can also affect beneficial insects. When applying DE, it's a good idea to wear a mask and eye protection to avoid inhaling the powder or getting it in your eyes.

While pests and diseases may be the least fun part of gardening (and certainly the least fun part to write about!), try not to get overly focused on what can go wrong. Instead, focus on making the healthiest ecosystem you can, and learn by observing your garden to see what works and what doesn't. Gardening is both process and product.

t's time to get growing! In this next section, I've selected plants that are generally considered easy to grow (lettuce, radishes, beans) for beginners and plants that you're likely to *want* to grow in your garden as a beginner, even if they might be a bit more of a challenge (broccoli, tomatoes). I've omitted crops such as cauliflower and celery that are thought to be rather difficult because of their specific requirements. (But of course there's nothing stopping you from giving anything you want a try—it's perfectly fine to have an experimental area.) Happy gardening!

PART TWO

PLANT PROFILES

AMARANTH, RED-LEAF

Amaranthus tricolor

FAMILY:	Amaranthaceae
SEASON:	Warm weather, summer
PROPAGATION:	Sow directly in the garden
PLANTING DEPTH:	⅛ inch (3 mm)
SOIL:	Well-drained soil with added compost
SUN:	Full
SOIL TEMPERATURE:	65° to 75°F (18 to 24°C)
SPACING:	Thin plants to 6 inches (15 cm) apart or grow more thickly for baby greens.
GROWING:	Easy to grow, red-leaf amaranth is a heat- and drought-tolerant plant, but it would prefer to stay evenly watered.
HARVEST:	Harvest as baby or full-size greens. Snip off the outside leaves to give the smaller inner leaves time to mature, then continue to harvest as the newer leaves grow.
CONTAINERS:	Red-leaf amaranth grows well in containers and works particularly well when harvested as a baby green.

You may be familiar with amaranth as an ancient grain, but some varieties are grown primarily for their leaves, like this one. While lettuce is a cool-weather crop that tends to bolt (go to seed) in hot weather, red-leaf amaranth is heat tolerant, making it ideal for your summer salad bowl or perfect for the garden of anyone who lives in a warm climate. Also known as Chinese multicolor spinach or red callaloo, this leafy green is high in protein, micronutrients, and fiber and is somewhat spinach-like in flavor (arguably even tastier). It has stunning variegated green-and-red leaves that recall the inedible ornamental plant coleus in appearance. Red-leaf amaranth can be eaten raw or cooked.

Amaranth, Red-Leaf   77

A R U G U L A
(R O C K E T)

Eruca sativa, Diplotaxis tenuifolia

FAMILY:	Brassicaceae
SEASON:	Cool weather, spring, fall
PROPAGATION:	Sow directly in the garden or start indoors from seed
PLANTING DEPTH:	⅛ to ¼ inch (3 to 6 mm)
SOIL:	Well-drained soil with added compost
SUN:	Full sun to part shade
SOIL TEMPERATURE:	40° to 50°F for germination (4° to 10°C)
SPACING:	Thin to 6 inches (15 cm) apart
GROWING:	For a consistent harvest, sow successively every 2 weeks while the temperatures remain cool. As the weather warms, arugula has a tendency to bolt, or go to seed, making the leaves even spicier. You can pinch off the flowers to slow bolting. To further reduce heat stress on the plant, keep up with watering and provide some shade.
HARVEST:	You will be able to start harvesting arugula in just a few weeks, when the leaves are about 3 inches (8 cm) long. Snip off the outside leaves to give the smaller inner leaves time to mature. Then you can continue to harvest as the newer leaves grow.

CONTAINERS: Arugula makes a great container plant. You can also sow the seeds more thickly and harvest as a baby green.

Super tasty, nutrient dense, and one of the easiest crops to grow, arugula is a must-have for any gardener, beginner or expert. Its peppery leaves enliven a salad, and it is equally good made into a pesto or mounded atop a pizza just out of the oven.

Arugula is a member of the brassica family, which includes broccoli, bok choy, cabbage, Brussels sprouts, kale, and other healthy favorites. For your garden, you can choose from either standard or wild varieties. The wild varieties have more deeply lobed leaves with fine indentations, while the standard varieties have more rounded, less indented leaves. In warmer climates, look for heat-tolerant varieties.

Arugula (Rocket)

BASIL

Ocimum basilicum and other species

FAMILY:	Lamiaceae
SEASON:	Warm weather, summer
PROPAGATION:	Sow directly in the garden or start indoors from seed
PLANTING DEPTH:	¼ inch (6 mm)
SOIL:	Well-drained soil with added compost
SUN:	Full sun
SOIL TEMPERATURE:	70° to 85°F (21° to 29°C)
SPACING:	8 to 12 inches (20 to 30 cm) apart
GROWING:	Basil is a trouble-free crop that likes to stay moist. Regular harvests can make the plant bushier and more productive. To allow the basil to mature properly and for sufficient airflow, don't be tempted to space your plants too closely together.
HARVEST:	Instead of just picking off leaves from the stem, pinch the whole stem back, leaving at least one pair of leaves so that it can regrow. Fresh basil sprigs can be placed in a glass of water on the counter. Basil can be dried for longer storage or made into pesto and frozen for later use.
CONTAINERS:	Basil is a superb container plant. For best results, grow only one plant per container.

One of the most popular garden herbs and incredibly easy to grow, basil has a spicy, anise-like flavor and an unforgettable aroma. If you're familiar with only sweet Italian basil, you're in for a treat, because there are countless other kinds, notably Thai and holy basil; lemon, lime, and cinnamon basil; purple basils; small-leafed bush basils; and even large-leafed lettuce basil. There's really a whole world of basil—and a whole world of cuisines that use basil—to explore.

Native to India and other regions of Asia, this member of the mint family is a warm-weather crop that is very sensitive to lower temperatures; it will be damaged if the mercury drops below 50°F (10°C), so you really want to make sure your nights—and your soil temps—are warm enough before your basil plant goes out to the garden. It makes a good companion plant for tomatoes, as its scent may deter pests.

To prevent basil from going to seed, pinch off any flower buds before they open. Once basil does go to seed, however, there are a number of varieties that produce beautiful flowers (which are very attractive to pollinators). Cardinal and Siam Queen are particularly lovely.

BEANS

Phaseolus spp., *Vigna* spp.

FAMILY:	Fabaceae
SEASON:	Warm weather, summer
PROPAGATION:	Sow directly in the garden
PLANTING DEPTH:	1 inch (2.5 cm)
SOIL:	Well-drained soil
SUN:	Full sun
SOIL TEMPERATURE:	70° to 90°F (21° to 32°C)
SPACING:	Spacing requirements can vary, so follow the packet instructions. For bush beans, plant generally 2 to 4 inches (5 to 10 cm) apart in rows 18 to 24 inches (46 to 61 cm) apart. For pole beans, plant a few beans spaced around each pole or support structure.
GROWING:	A warm-weather crop, beans should be started only when the soil temperature is right. Beans are one of those crops best sown directly in the ground or in their final container. For improved growth and increased yields, dust the seeds with a legume inoculant before planting. Inoculants are available through seed companies and nurseries.

For bush beans, remember that the harvest for most varieties will happen over a short period of time. If that's the case for the beans you're growing, stagger your plantings, starting new seeds every 2 to 3 weeks, so you don't end up with a glut of beans all at the same time.

Beans 83

For pole beans, train the plants on a trellis, pole, or other support as they grow.

Fertilize the plants after blooming. Avoid fertilizers that are high in nitrogen because they increase leafy growth instead of bean production.

HARVEST: Regular picking will promote greater production. Harvest when the beans reach the size indicated on the packet. Beans that are left on the plant too long can become tough. (The exception to this would be beans that you plan to dry; these should be left on the plant until the pods are dry.)

CONTAINERS: Bush beans are great for containers.

Native mostly to Central and South America, beans are one of the most satisfying and delicious crops to grow. They grow quickly, produce prodigiously, and are mostly fuss-free. While you can choose among countless varieties of snap beans (string beans), filet beans (haricots verts), dry beans, broad beans (such as limas and favas), and long beans, bean plants have two main growing styles: bush and pole. When shopping for seeds, be sure to check out which style you're buying. While the form in which they grow is different, their growing requirements are the same.

Bush beans stay compact and small, like a bush, and most varieties will produce a flush of beans in a short period of time. Bush beans are a good choice for containers because of their size.

Pole beans are vining (think: "Jack and the Beanstalk") and need a supportive structure to grow on. They will also keep on producing throughout the growing season. While bush beans are a more traditional choice for container planting, you can grow pole beans this way, too, as long as you provide them with something to climb on. If you live in a hot climate and struggle to find bean varieties that work for you, check out yardlong beans (a type of pole bean), some of which can indeed reach 3 feet (1 m) long.

For varieties, try Provider (bush), Cosmos (bush), Maxibel French Filet (bush), and Kentucky Wonder (pole). Two favorite yardlong beans are Chinese Red Noodle (pole) and Chinese Mosaic (pole).

BEETS

Beta vulgaris

FAMILY:	Amaranthaceae
SEASON:	Cool weather, spring, fall
PROPAGATION:	Sow directly in the garden or start indoors from seed
PLANTING DEPTH:	½ inch (1.3 cm)
SOIL:	Well-drained sandy or light soil with added compost
SUN:	Full sun to part shade
SOIL TEMPERATURE:	50°F (10°C)
SPACING:	Thin to 4 inches (10 cm) apart
GROWING:	Each seed is actually a cluster of several seeds, so once the plants are a few inches tall, keep only the strongest plant in the group. You can snip the others off at soil level and use them as baby greens. Beets like cool, moist conditions, so water regularly and mulch well to help maintain moisture levels. Use a balanced fertilizer or one higher in phosphorus and potassium than nitrogen, because high levels of nitrogen will promote leaf growth rather than root growth.
HARVEST:	For best flavor and texture, beets should be harvested when they reach maturity (this size will be indicated on the seed packet), typically when they're around the size of a golf ball or a little bigger.

CONTAINERS: Choose an 8- to 10-inch-deep (20 to 25 cm) container and sow the seeds directly.

While beets may be a divisive vegetable in terms of flavor, there's no arguing over their beauty and health benefits. They come in inky, rich jewel tones—deep ruby red, golden yellow—and even candy-striped, and both the greens and roots are edible. Beets are incredibly high in antioxidants, thanks to the betalains (the red compound that gives them their color) they contain. Beet greens are a superfood as well, so don't overlook them—you can harvest a few leaves at a time to cook before harvesting the beets themselves.

If you think beets taste like dirt, well, you're right. Scientists tell us that this is due to the presence of geosmin, an earthy- and musty-tasting compound produced by bacteria in the soil; a recent article suggests that beets may also produce this compound on their own. Try the Chiogga, Red Ace, Bull's Blood (for baby greens), and Boldor varieties.

BORAGE

Borago officinalis

FAMILY:	Boraginaceae
SEASON:	Warm weather, spring, summer
PROPAGATION:	Sow directly in the garden
PLANTING DEPTH:	½ inch (1.3 cm)
SOIL:	Average to poor well-drained soil
SUN:	Full sun to part shade
SOIL TEMPERATURE:	60° to 70°F (15° to 21°C)
SPACING:	Thin to 12 inches (30 cm) apart
GROWING:	Because of borage's long taproot, sowing it directly in the garden rather than transplanting it is recommended. The plant self-seeds, so you don't need to replant it the next year, but you may need to thin it out or be judicious about its placement in the garden.
HARVEST:	Harvest flowers as needed.
CONTAINERS:	Choose a container at least 12 inches (30 cm) deep to accommodate borage's long taproot.

With nodding star-shaped blue flowers that attract bees and beneficial insects, borage is an herb you might not be familiar with—but should be! It has a long history of use in folk medicine and is thought to repel tomato hornworms, cabbage worms, and other insect pests. The flowers are edible and taste a bit like cucumbers; they can be added to salads and drinks or even candied. When the plant gets older, the leaves and stems get quite prickly, so wear gloves when handling. Borage is unfussy and grows well in most soils, as long as they're well drained. It's worth growing for the good it will do for bees—and for its lovely flowers.

BROCCOLI

Brassica oleracea

FAMILY:	Brassicaceae
SEASON:	Cool weather, spring, fall
PROPAGATION:	Start indoors or buy transplants
PLANTING DEPTH:	¼ to ½ inch (6 to 13 mm)
SOIL:	Well-drained soil with added compost
SUN:	Full sun
SOIL TEMPERATURE:	45° to 85°F (7° to 29°C)
SPACING:	18 inches (46 cm) apart in rows 24 to 36 inches (61 to 91 cm) apart
GROWING:	For a spring crop, start seeds indoors 6 to 8 weeks before the last frost, and transplant into the garden about 2 weeks before the last frost. For a fall crop, start seeds 10 to 12 weeks before your average first frost date. Mulch well and provide consistent watering, though avoid getting water on the head itself. If temperatures remain cool, broccoli plants can produce additional heads from side shoots.
HARVEST:	Harvest fully formed heads when the buds are still tight; if the buds start to open (you'll see a hint of yellow), harvest immediately. Use a sharp knife to avoid stem damage.

CONTAINERS: Broccoli can be grown in containers, but the combination of growing requirements plus the need for a large container (and only one plant per pot) might not make it the best choice for a small space.

Broccoli can be a bit of a challenging crop to grow well because it requires quite cool conditions (60° to 70°F/15° to 21°C) over an extended period of time, a growing environment that not all gardeners will be able to provide. A head of broccoli is really a cluster of unopened flower buds, and as temperatures warm up to 80°F (26°C) and higher, those flowers will open, causing the plant to bolt. If you don't succeed with a spring crop, you may have more luck in the fall if you start the seeds indoors in early to mid-summer. Another alternative is to grow mini or sprouting broccoli, which has a shorter period to maturity, though some varieties require growing conditions below 50°F (10°C) for a period of time (which will be specified on the seed packet) to produce florets. Early-sprouting varieties, also known as summer-sprouting varieties, do not have this requirement.

Your local extension office may be able to suggest varieties that grow well in your area. Some ideas include Calabrese, Di Cicco, and Waltham. Also explore Chinese broccoli (gai lan) and broccoli rabe.

CABBAGE

Brassica oleracea

FAMILY:	Brassicaceae
SEASON:	Cool weather, spring, fall
PROPAGATION:	Start indoors from seed, buy transplants, sow directly in the garden
PLANTING DEPTH:	¼ inch (6 mm)
SOIL:	Fertile, slightly acidic to pH-neutral soil with added compost
SUN:	Full sun to part shade (in warmer climates)
SOIL TEMPERATURE:	75°F (24°C) for germination, then 60° to 65°F (16° to 18°C)
SPACING:	Approximately 18 inches (46 cm) apart
GROWING:	Plant seedlings of early varieties in the garden in spring, about 2 weeks before the last frost. Direct-sow late varieties about 90 days before the first frost. Mulch well to retain soil moisture and weed carefully to avoid disturbing the plant's shallow root system. Supplement with a balanced fertilizer. Cabbages are very attractive to insect pests, including flea beetles, cabbage worms, and cabbage loopers. See page 66 for advice on prevention and management.
HARVEST:	Harvest with a sharp knife once heads reach the desired size and are firm. The plant can produce additional heads if the outer leaves and stem are left intact.

CONTAINERS: Not recommended

Perfect for slaws, salads, sauerkraut, and more, cabbage is sweet, crunchy, and high in nutrients.

Whether you prefer green, red, or savoy, this cool-weather crop needs rich soil and sufficient nutrients to thrive. You should be able to get two harvests per year, one in the spring and one in the fall, and there are varieties designed for early (spring) harvest and late (fall to winter) harvest. Select your varieties accordingly. Late cabbages store well in a root cellar or other cool, dry places. If you live somewhere with a mild winter, you may be able to grow them throughout the winter. The ideal temperature range for growing cabbage is between 60° and 70°F (15° and 21°C).

Because of the risk of soilborne diseases, practice good crop rotation (page 35). Brassicas are often grown following a bean crop, which sets nitrogen in the soil.

CABBAGE, CHINESE (NAPA)

Brassica rapa

FAMILY:	Brassicaceae
SEASON:	Cool weather, spring, fall
PROPAGATION:	Start indoors from seed, buy transplants, sow directly in the garden
PLANTING DEPTH:	¼ to ½ inch (6 to 13 mm)
SOIL:	Fertile, slightly acidic to pH-neutral soil with added compost
SUN:	Full sun to part shade
SOIL TEMPERATURE:	75°F (24°C) for germination, then 60° to 65°F (16° to 18°C)
SPACING:	Approximately 15 inches (38 cm) apart
GROWING:	For a spring crop, transplant seedlings into the garden around the last frost date, but if temperatures remain under 50°F (10°C) at night for more than a few days, the plant may bolt. For a fall crop, direct-sow in midsummer, about 10 to 12 weeks before the first frost. You can grow Chinese cabbage as a successional crop, planting a few seeds every few weeks.
HARVEST:	Harvest when the head feels firm, using a sharp knife to cut the head off at the base.

CONTAINERS: It's possible, but the need for a large container (around 5 gallons/22 L per plant) might not make it the best choice for a small space.

Whether for stir-fries, kimchi, soups, or just eaten raw, Chinese cabbage—also known as napa cabbage—is a delicious addition to your garden. It has a slightly mustardy flavor and a light, crisp texture. More heat tolerant than European cabbage varieties (see page 92), it has similar growing requirements but a slightly shorter period to maturity. Like those European varieties, you can plant both a spring crop and a fall crop, but it often performs best as a fall crop as late-summer temperatures begin to dip and the day length shortens. Spring plants are more prone to bolting in cold temperatures. Interesting tidbit: Napa cabbage has nothing to do with Napa Valley; the name is thought to come from the Japanese dialect word *nappa*, meaning "greens."

CARROTS

Daucus carota

FAMILY:	Apiaceae
SEASON:	Cool weather, spring, fall
PROPAGATION:	Sow directly in the garden
PLANTING DEPTH:	¼ inch (6 mm)
SOIL:	Loose, sandy soil
SUN:	Full sun to part shade
SOIL TEMPERATURE:	60° to 70°F (16° to 21°C) for best results
SPACING:	Thin to 2 inches (5 cm) apart in rows 12 inches (30 cm) apart
GROWING:	Carrot seeds are very tiny, making them a challenge to sow thinly, but do your best and take your time. Some experts advise mixing the seeds with a little bit of sand or fine soil to help. Cover the seeds with a thin layer of fine soil and keep them moist. Seeds will germinate in anywhere between 5 and 21 days depending on how warm the soil is. The most important thing is not to let the soil dry out during this time.
	Because carrots are susceptible to a pest called the carrot rust fly, cover them with row covers to protect them.
	To thin, snip the seedling at the base to avoid disrupting the roots of the other carrots.

HARVEST: To determine readiness for harvest, brush aside the soil around the top of the carrot to gauge its diameter. Depending on the variety, harvest-ready carrots could be anywhere from ½ to 2 inches (1.3 to 5 cm) across.

CONTAINERS: Choose containers at least 12 inches (30 cm) deep.

If you've only ever eaten supermarket carrots, you're in for a delight. The flavor of a homegrown carrot is incomparable, and the incredible variety available will have you wanting *all the carrots*. There are short, sweet, stubby carrots; purple carrots with yellow or orange interiors; purple carrots that are as dark as beets; red carrots; yellow carrots; true baby carrots; even carrots that grow up to 3 feet (1 m) long. Check out Little Finger, Cosmic Purple, and New Kuroda.

If there's one thing a carrot wants, it's loose soil, so it's an ideal crop for raised beds. If you're not growing in a raised bed, loosen the soil, removing any rocks and sticks and breaking up big clumps. Compost and leaf mold can be added to improve drainage. If you've got only heavy clay soil, all is not lost: look for carrot varieties bred to tolerate more challenging soil conditions.

Carrots become sweeter in cool weather and can even withstand some frost, which signals them to start storing sugars in the root. If your carrots are bitter, it's possible they were either harvested too early or the growing temperatures were too hot.

CHIVES

Allium schoenoprasum

FAMILY:	Amaryllidaceae
SEASON:	n/a
PROPAGATION:	Start indoors from seed, buy transplants or obtain divisions, sow directly in the garden
PLANTING DEPTH:	¼ inch (6 mm)
SOIL:	Well-drained soil with added compost
SUN:	Full sun to part shade
SOIL TEMPERATURE:	65° to 70°F (18° to 21°C) for germination
SPACING:	Thin to 6 inches (15 cm) apart
GROWING:	Chives are fairly easy to start from seed, whether indoors or directly in the garden, but they take a little while to get established. It's easier to get a division from a neighbor or pick up a started plant or two. If sowing directly, plant the seeds as soon as the soil warms up to about 65°F (18°C). Established chive plants are tolerant of a range of growing conditions.
HARVEST:	Snip chives at the base of the plant. The flowers can be harvested just after they open. Keep moist, particularly in warm temperatures and until the plants are well established in their new location.

CONTAINERS: Chives are great for containers. Your best bet is to buy a started plant. You can even grow them on a very sunny windowsill (south-facing in the Northern Hemisphere and north-facing in the Southern Hemisphere).

A member of the lily family, chives are delicious snipped into scrambled eggs, tossed with potato salad or sautéed mushrooms, or sprinkled on a dish just before serving to give a hint of grassy onion flavor. The plant is perennial, which means it will come back each year (if the winters are mild where you are, it may overwinter). Both the hollow-stemmed leaves and the pretty purple flowers are edible. Even better, the flowers are loved by bees. This easy-to-grow plant grows in clumps, which you should divide every few years to prevent overcrowding. Division is also a way of propagating the plants. It's thought that chives deter carrot rust flies (see page 96).

Garlic chives (*Allium tuberosum*), a relative of *A. schoenoprasum*, are flat and grasslike in appearance and, as the name suggests, have a more garlicky flavor.

CILANTRO (CORIANDER)

Coriandrum sativum

FAMILY:	Apiaceae
SEASON:	Cool weather, spring, fall
PROPAGATION:	Sow directly in the garden
PLANTING DEPTH:	½ inch (1.3 cm)
SOIL:	Well-drained soil with added compost
SUN:	Full sun
SOIL TEMPERATURE:	65° to 70°F (18 to 21°C)
SPACING:	1 to 2 inches (2.5 to 5 cm) apart in rows 3 to 4 inches (8 to 10 cm) apart
GROWING:	Because cilantro doesn't transplant well, sow it directly in the garden in early spring and in the fall. The challenge with growing cilantro is its tendency to bolt, or go to seed. Look for slow-bolting varieties, and plant successively to have a harvest throughout the season. Keeping the plant well watered can help slow bolting, as can mulching.
HARVEST:	Harvest as needed by snipping the stems at the base of the plant. Seeds can either be harvested fresh, when they are immature, or left on the plant until they dry.

CONTAINERS: Cilantro is great for containers; just be sure to plant the seed in the final container you plan to grow it in to avoid having to transplant it.

A cool-season crop, cilantro is an herb integral to a range of cuisines around the world, including Latin American, Caribbean, Southeast Asian, and East Asian. *Cilantro*, the name commonly used in North America to refer to the fresh herb, is the Spanish word for "coriander," and indeed, in many other parts of the English-speaking world, *coriander* is the name given to both the leafy plant and its seed. In the US, the word *coriander* is often reserved for the plant's seed, a warm, floral, citrusy spice typically used ground.

Many people dislike cilantro because it tastes soapy to them, and there's a bit of a genetic component to this; however, it's believed that when the herb is crushed, as it is in a sofrito or chimichurri, it becomes more palatable to some individuals. For me, though, it's as invaluable and versatile as parsley for my cooking, and I'd never be without it.

Cilantro (Coriander)

COLLARD GREENS

Brassica oleracea

FAMILY:	Brassicaceae
SEASON:	Cool weather, spring, fall, early winter
PROPAGATION:	Start indoors from seed or sow directly in the garden
PLANTING DEPTH:	½ inch (1.3 cm)
SOIL:	Well-drained soil with added compost
SUN:	Full sun to part shade
SOIL TEMPERATURE:	50° to 75°F (10° to 24°C)
SPACING:	If direct sowing, thin plants to 12 inches (30 cm) apart in rows 24 to 36 inches (61 to 91 cm) apart
GROWING:	For a spring crop, collard greens can be started indoors and transplanted to the garden in early spring. For a fall crop, plant 2½ to 3 months before the first frost. Mulch well to prolong the growing season into winter. Keep consistently moist.
HARVEST:	Harvest outer leaves first to allow the smaller, inner leaves time to mature.
CONTAINERS:	Collard greens can be grown in large containers (one plant per 5-gallon/22 L pot) but might not be the best choice for a small space.

There are few things as delicious as stewed collard greens (even without the traditional ham hock or bacon). Collards are very mild; in fact, if you tend to find green leafy vegetables bitter and you've never tried collards, you might just find they're your new favorite greens. Collards are a kind of cabbage that does not form a head. They date back to the ancient Greeks and are a staple in the southern US, where they are particularly well suited to the region's mild winters, but they also grow well in northern climates.

Like other cruciferous greens, collards are incredibly good for you: they're high in vitamins K and C, calcium, fiber, iron, and other nutrients. They can be eaten raw or cooked and are grown similarly to kale. While collard greens prefer cooler temperatures, they can tolerate more warmth than kale and can continue to produce if winters are mild. A frost can make them sweeter!

CORN

Zea mays

FAMILY:	Poaceae
SEASON:	Warm weather, summer
PROPAGATION:	Sow directly from seed
PLANTING DEPTH:	1 inch (2.5 cm)
SOIL:	Well-drained fertile soil with added compost
SUN:	Full sun
SOIL TEMPERATURE:	60°F (16°C)
SPACING:	Thin to 6 to 8 inches (15 to 20 cm) apart in rows about 36 inches (91 cm) apart
GROWING:	Corn is a heavy feeder, requires very fertile soil, and needs quite a bit of water. In the fall, prepare the bed for the next year by incorporating compost into the soil. Corn has a shallow root system, so mulching in mounds can help stabilize the plants and retain moisture. In addition, weed carefully to avoid disturbing the roots. Supplement with a high-nitrogen fertilizer.
HARVEST:	There are some tricks to knowing when corn is ready for harvest. When corn enters the milk stage, about 17 to 20 days after the cornsilk appears, it is ready for picking. One common indicator is that the silks will turn brown and dry out. The kernels will also feel full: if you pull

down the husk and pierce the kernels with your fingernail and a milky liquid comes out, put a pot of water on the stove—it's ready! If you miss this window, the corn will not be as sweet.

CONTAINERS: Not recommended

Sweet corn is one of the most delicious garden crops, and because the sugar content in corn drops so quickly after harvest, you really haven't had corn until you've had fresh-picked sweet corn. It does require quite a large space to grow, so depending on the size of your garden plot, it might not be for you. Corn is wind pollinated, and each individual kernel needs to be pollinated, so plant in blocks of at least four rows to ensure sufficient pollination. Think carefully about its placement, too—because it gets so tall, it can limit the sunlight that reaches neighboring plants.

CUCUMBERS

Cucumis sativus

FAMILY:	Cucurbitaceae
SEASON:	Warm weather, summer
PROPAGATION:	Sow directly in the garden or start indoors from seed
PLANTING DEPTH:	½ inch (1.3 cm)
SOIL:	Well-drained fertile soil with added compost
SUN:	Full sun
SOIL TEMPERATURE:	70°F (21°C)
SPACING:	Thin to 12 inches (30 cm) apart in rows 5 to 6 feet (1.5 to 1.8 m) apart
GROWING:	While common advice is to sow cucumbers directly because they don't transplant well, you *can* start them from seed. Just keep seedlings moist, and wait until the soil temperature reaches at least 70°F (21°C) before you transplant them to the garden, being careful not to disturb the roots too much as you do. While cucumbers are prone to a number of pests and diseases, including powdery mildew (see page 65), many varieties have been bred for disease resistance. Good gardening hygiene, including trellising, keeping up with watering, correct spacing (which increases airflow), beneficial insects, and row covers can all help.

HARVEST: The seed packet will generally provide guidance on how long a mature cucumber will be. It varies, depending on whether it's a kind for slicing or pickling. Regular picking hastens ripening of other cucumbers and spurs production.

CONTAINERS: Bush varieties are best for containers, but if you provide sufficient support, you can also grow vining types.

One of the great pleasures of the summer garden is a cucumber, tomato, and basil salad. That, and a crunchy refrigerator pickle made with your own dill. Though you might associate cucumbers with coolness because of the characteristics of the fruit, they're firmly a warm-weather crop and grow prodigiously in summer. Because they are so productive, they are one of the most enjoyable crops for a beginner to grow.

The watery texture of cucumber flesh gives you a hint as to how to care for it. Cucumber plants are thirsty, and if you grow them in containers, you might find yourself watering at least once a day on hot days. They're also heavy feeders, so plant them in rich soil and supplement with a balanced fertilizer, if needed.

As with beans, there are two kinds: bush and vining. **Bush varieties** stay compact, while **vining varieties** will need a trellis, fence, or other support structure to grow on. Vining cucumber plants can get *big*, reaching 6 to 8 feet (1.8 to 2.4 m) tall.

DILL

Anethum graveolens

FAMILY:	Apiaceae
SEASON:	Cool weather, spring, fall
PROPAGATION:	Start indoors from seed, sow directly in the garden
PLANTING DEPTH:	⅛ inch (3 mm)
SOIL:	Loose, well-drained soil
SUN:	Full sun
SOIL TEMPERATURE:	60° to 65°F (16° to 18°F)
SPACING:	4 inches (10 cm) apart in rows 9 to 12 inches (23 to 30 cm) apart
GROWING:	If you start dill indoors from seed, transplant it carefully because it does not like its roots disturbed. Otherwise, direct-sow in the garden after the last frost date. Because dill goes to seed quickly, you can sow successively every few weeks for a continuous harvest. Dill is an annual, but if left to go to seed, the plant can reseed itself, producing a new crop on its own.
HARVEST:	Harvest the leaves from the outside of the plant to allow the smaller leaves in the center of the plant to mature.
CONTAINERS:	Fernleaf dill is ideal for containers.

How appropriate that cucumbers and dill sit next to each other in this book, because they're perfect partners (think: pickles and tzatziki). Dill also is great with fish, cream sauces, potatoes, and many other foods. As with cilantro (see page 100), you can use both the leaves and the seeds of the dill plant for cooking. Beyond its wonderful flavor, there's even more reason to make space for it in your garden: the plant can attract hoverflies, a beneficial insect. Dill grows quickly and is not fussy, but it will bolt in hot temperatures. Try the Fernleaf and Dukat varieties.

EDAMAME

Glycine max

FAMILY:	Fabaceae
SEASON:	Warm weather, summer
PROPAGATION:	Sow directly in the garden
PLANTING DEPTH:	1 inch (2.5 cm)
SOIL:	Well-drained soil with added compost
SUN:	Full sun
SOIL TEMPERATURE:	65°F (18°C)
SPACING:	Thin to 4 to 6 inches (10 to 15 cm) apart in rows 12 to 18 inches (30 to 46 cm) apart
GROWING:	Soybeans love warm weather, so sow directly once any threat of frost has passed. Mulch young plants to help retain moisture and keep weeds under control. Because the pods will ripen all at once, stagger your plantings every 2 weeks to provide a continuous harvest. Avoid fertilizers that are high in nitrogen because they can lead to more leafy growth instead of bean production.
HARVEST:	When the pods reach maturity, snip them off the plant, or harvest the whole plant. The beans must be cooked before being eaten. Steam or boil them, remove them from their pods, then toss them into salads and stir-fries—or just eat them sprinkled with a little sea salt.

CONTAINERS: Soybean plants are relatively small (1 to 3 feet/30 to 91 cm tall), so they're a good option for containers.

You've probably enjoyed a bowl of steamed edamame at a Japanese restaurant, but have you ever thought of growing it? Edamame are simply young soybeans, and they can be a fun addition to the garden. What's more, they're a complete protein, high in fiber, and a great source of iron. They do require a long growing season, which might not be possible in all areas, but there are early-maturing varieties, such as Envy and Chiba. Consider checking with your local extension office for recommendations, or look for early varieties on seed company websites.

E G G P L A N T

Solanum melongena

FAMILY:	Solanaceae
SEASON:	Warm weather, summer
PROPAGATION:	Start indoors from seed
PLANTING DEPTH:	¼ inch (6 mm)
SOIL:	Well-drained soil with added compost
SUN:	Full sun
SOIL TEMPERATURE:	80° to 90°F (27° to 32°C) for germination, but can be lower thereafter
SPACING:	18 to 24 inches (46 to 61 cm) apart in rows at least 36 inches (91 cm) apart
GROWING:	Because eggplant like warmth, don't rush them out into the garden. Wait until late spring/early summer to plant your seedlings; daytime temps should be at least 70°F (21°C), and nights shouldn't dip below 60°F (15°C). It can be helpful to add a tomato cage or stakes for support, as the fruits are heavy. Because of the risk of flea beetles (see page 68) and Colorado potato beetles (see page 67), consider using a row cover until the transplants are established. Eggplant needs consistent irrigation, so mulch to help retain moisture and don't let the soil dry out entirely.
HARVEST:	To increase production, pick regularly. Eggplant can be picked before they reach full size—they should be firm with glossy skin. Use shears or garden scissors.

CONTAINERS: Eggplant is great in containers. Look for mini varieties like Fairy Tale and Patio Baby.

Depending on where you live, you might hear a variation of one of these two statements from fellow gardeners regarding eggplants: "I can't grow eggplant; eggplant is so unpredictable," or "Eggplant is easy to grow." Eggplant is a warm-weather plant, but it's sensitive to too-hot temps, so it's easier to grow in climates that can accommodate its needs. Knowing those needs may help you decide whether you'd like to give it a try; fortunately, it can be a bit more forgiving in pots, and there are plenty of beautiful varieties ideal for container gardening.

What's wonderful about the eggplant is its diversity and how widely it is grown around the world. In East Asia, Southeast Asia, Africa, the Caribbean, the Middle East, the Mediterranean, and the Americas, eggplant has been incorporated in varied cuisines, so you'll have no shortage of recipes to use it in. The most common types of seeds that home gardeners will find are Asian, Italian, and mini varieties. If you find eggplant bitter, I've noticed that Italian types with light purple (as opposed to dark purple-black) skin tend to be milder. The Asian varieties tend to be mild as well. Try Rosita, Dancer, Nagasaki Long, Fairy Tale, or Patio Baby.

GARLIC

Allium sativum

FAMILY:	Amaryllidaceae
SEASON:	Warm weather, spring, summer
PROPAGATION:	Sow directly in the garden
PLANTING DEPTH:	2 to 3 inches (5 to 8 cm)
SOIL:	Well-drained soil with added compost
SUN:	Full sun to part shade
SOIL TEMPERATURE:	n/a
SPACING:	6 inches (15 cm) apart and in rows 1 to 2 feet (30 to 61 cm) apart
GROWING:	Separate but do not peel the cloves before planting. In autumn, sometime between the first frost date and November, plant one clove per hole, root end facing down. Cover with several inches of straw or leaves to provide a layer of insulation over the winter. In spring, after the ground has warmed up, remove the layer of straw and add a layer of compost to retain moisture and suppress weeds. Keep evenly watered and well weeded. If you are growing hardneck garlic, it will send up a long stem known as a scape, which will spiral. At that point, it should be cut off. The scape is edible—in fact, it's delicious in stir-fries, and you can make a pesto out of it.

Garlic

Veg Out

HARVEST: Garlic is ready for harvest when a few of the bottom leaves start to turn yellow and brown. To avoid bruising the garlic (which will affect how long it will keep in storage), carefully dig up the heads and, with your hands, gently remove excess soil from the long roots, but do not cut them. The bulbs will need to cure for about 2 weeks in a warm, dry, well-ventilated spot. After they are cured, you can trim the stems and roots and store in a cool, dry location.

CONTAINERS: Garlic can be grown in pots, and it can also be grown in containers just for its leaves.

Homegrown garlic is light-years better than the sad, sprouting, often dried-out heads you find at the supermarket. It's easy to grow but does require a bit of advance planning. The bulbs need time to establish a root system, so garlic is generally planted in the fall for harvest the following summer. This means that if you've started planning your first garden in winter, it might be too late to include garlic, depending on your climate. If you have mild winters, though, you can plant in early winter or even as late as early spring.

There are three main kinds of garlic: hardneck/stiffneck, softneck, and elephant. Hardneck garlic has a hard central stem around which the cloves form. This variety is cold hardy and so is a good choice in cooler climates. Softneck garlic has a flexible, braidable stem and is less cold hardy, making it a better choice for warmer locations. Related to leeks, elephant garlic produces very large heads that are quite mild in flavor.

Garlic from the supermarket is not suitable for planting in the garden—it may have been treated to prevent sprouting, and you can't be certain it's disease-free. Buy seed garlic (which comes in bulbs) from a seed company, local nursery, or other reputable supplier.

KALE

Brassica oleracea

FAMILY:	Brassicaceae
SEASON:	Cool weather, spring, fall, winter
PROPAGATION:	Start indoors from seed, sow directly in the garden
PLANTING DEPTH:	½ inch (1.3 cm)
SOIL:	Well-drained soil with added compost
SUN:	Full sun to part shade
SOIL TEMPERATURE:	50° to 75°F (10° to 24°C)
SPACING:	If direct-seeding, thin plants to 12 inches (30 cm) apart.
GROWING:	For a spring crop, kale can be started indoors and transplanted to the garden in early spring. For a fall crop, plant about 3 months before the first frost. Mulch well to prolong the length of the growing season into winter. Keep consistently moist. Bolting, which happens in hot weather and when plants are stressed, makes the plants bitter.
HARVEST:	Harvest outer leaves first to allow the smaller inner leaves time to mature. For baby greens, sow more thickly and harvest when the leaves reach the desired size.
CONTAINERS:	Kale is great in a container, particularly when harvested young as a baby green.

At one point in recent memory, kale was considered little more than a depressing restaurant garnish, sometimes paired with a lemon wedge of questionable freshness. But for a while now, things have been looking up for kale, and it's been having a good run: kale salads, kale smoothies, kale chips, kale stir-fries, kale *everything*. I'm on board with that, because kale is not only tasty but a nutritional powerhouse. I like it either blended raw in a smoothie or cooked until it's meltingly tender. It's a great addition to the garden because it will still be there when most other crops are but a sweet memory of warmer times. In fact, it gets even sweeter after a frost. Like collard greens, kale is a nonheading cabbage.

If you dislike the texture of curly-leafed kale, try growing lacinato kale (also known as Tuscan or dinosaur kale), which has long, wrinkled, blue-green leaves. Or experiment with Portuguese kale, which is similar to collards and essential for a comforting bowl of caldo verde.

LAVENDER

Lavandula angustifolia

FAMILY:	Lamiaceae
SEASON:	Warm weather, summer
PROPAGATION:	Start indoors from seed, buy transplants, use cuttings
PLANTING DEPTH:	⅛ inch (3 mm)
SOIL:	Well-drained slightly alkaline soil, preferably sandy
SUN:	Full sun
SOIL TEMPERATURE:	65° to 70°F (18° to 21°C)
SPACING:	12 inches (30 cm) apart
GROWING:	Lavender is challenging to grow from seed because it can be slow to germinate and takes a while to mature. If you'd like to get a head start, buy transplants or get cuttings from a friend. Lavender likes dry, hot conditions and good drainage (like Mediterranean conditions), so it's a great candidate for raised bed gardens. Plants need more water until they're established, but they are sturdy, tolerant plants. Lavender is perennial, so it will come back each year, but it will need some pruning.
HARVEST:	Harvest just before the flowers open. Hang to dry in a well-ventilated place, then store for use.

CONTAINERS: Lavender makes a nice container plant, especially if your garden doesn't have the free-draining sandy soil it loves.

With its distinctive, evocative fragrance and delicate beauty, lavender is a wonderful herb to add to the garden. While you can cut and dry arrangements to enjoy its relaxing scent year-round, the flower buds are delicious when finely ground and added to desserts (a favorite cake recipe is food writer Diana Henry's lemon and lavender cake), made into a simple syrup or tea, or added to a spice mixture such as herbes de Provence. Even better, it attracts pollinators to the garden.

While there are many different kinds of this Mediterranean herb—including *L. stoechas*, also known as Spanish lavender, and *L. dentata*, a tooth-leafed variety that is sometimes called French lavender—stick with *L. angustifolia*, known as English lavender, the most common variety, for culinary use. Munstead is a common culinary cultivar to look for. If you're going for just fragrance or wildlife, though, feel free to branch out!

Lavender 121

LETTUCE

Lactuca sativa

FAMILY:	Asteraceae
SEASON:	Cool weather, spring, fall
PROPAGATION:	Start indoors from seed, sow directly in the garden
PLANTING DEPTH:	⅛ to ¼ inch (3 to 6 mm)
SOIL:	Well-drained soil with added compost
SUN:	Full sun to part shade
SOIL TEMPERATURE:	45° to 80°F (7° to 27°C)
SPACING:	For a cut-and-come-again crop, 4 inches (10 cm) apart; for heads, 6 to 12 inches (15 to 30 cm), depending on the variety (check the packet instructions)
GROWING:	Lettuce needs very fertile soil and consistent (but not copious) watering. It is a cool-weather crop, so shade cloth or taller companion plants can help prolong the growing season when temperatures start to heat up. Once the lettuce forms a central stalk, it is bolting and will taste bitter. Plant every 1 to 2 weeks while temperatures are cool enough in the garden, then pick up again in late summer and fall.

Veg Out

HARVEST:	For baby greens, harvest the outside leaves first to give time for the smaller inner leaves to mature. For heads, harvest when it reaches a mature size (indicated on the packet). A solid head, such as iceberg, will feel firm.
CONTAINERS:	Baby lettuce greens are great for containers.

There are a dizzying number of lettuce varieties available. In one recent seed catalog, I counted fourteen pages of options. They can be roughly divided into a few different types: loose-leaf, which does not form a solid head; crisphead, which does form a solid head (think iceberg); romaine (also known as cos); and butterhead, which forms a loose head.

Lettuce is one of the easiest, fastest crops to grow, and to have a steady supply for salads, you'll want to keep planting it every 1 to 2 weeks during spring and fall. Some lettuce varieties to try are Black Seeded Simpson (loose-leaf), Parris Island Cos (romaine), and Buttercrunch (butterhead). Unless you live somewhere with particularly mild summers, you won't have lettuce during the hottest part of the growing season. During that period, try red-leaf amaranth (see page 76) or Malabar spinach (*Basella alba*), a vining plant that tastes similar to spinach (see page 155).

You have some options when it comes to how to grow lettuce: you can grow it a bit closer together and harvest it as baby greens, sometimes called cut-and-come-again lettuce, or space the plants farther apart, grow them to maturity, and harvest them whole— or you can do a mix of both! Most seed companies offer lettuce seed mixes that are perfect for baby greens.

MINT

Mentha spp.

FAMILY:	Lamiaceae
SEASON:	n/a
PROPAGATION:	Start indoors from seed, or obtain cuttings or divisions
PLANTING DEPTH:	Surface
SOIL:	Well-drained soil
SUN:	Part shade to full sun
SOIL TEMPERATURE:	55° to 75°F (13° to 24°C)
SPACING:	Containers are recommended; otherwise, 12 to 18 inches (30 to 46 cm) apart
GROWING:	Mint can be planted outdoors after the last frost. It needs a moderate amount of moisture. If you take a cutting or division at the end of the growing season, you can grow it indoors in winter. Mint can be cut back in autumn or early spring. If well mulched, you may be able to harvest a few leaves throughout the winter during warm spells.
HARVEST:	Harvest leaves or whole stems as needed. Use fresh, or dry for longer storage.
CONTAINERS:	Preferred, because of mint's invasive tendencies.

Mint is an ideal herb for the new gardener because it is so easy (almost *too* easy) to grow. As you might have guessed, there is a *but*. The *but* is that this perennial plant can spread and become invasive, so growing it in containers is usually recommended. There are various kinds of mint: peppermint is the kind typically used in teas, while spearmint is used in culinary applications both savory and sweet, everything from tabbouleh and pho to fruit salad and mojitos. Many aromatic mints exist, including chocolate mint, apple mint, and ginger mint. Because of mint's tendency to hybridize, it does not produce seeds that are true to type (meaning they will not produce a plant identical to the parent plant), so if you buy seeds, the package will most likely just say "mint," and you won't know what you've got until you plant it. To get a specific mint, buy started plants or get a cutting from a friend and experiment with propagation!

Even if you don't think you'll use a lot of mint, consider including a few pots in the garden, because it's said to repel insect pests.

OREGANO

Origanum spp.

FAMILY:	Lamiaceae
SEASON:	Warm weather, summer
PROPAGATION:	Start indoors from seed, buy transplants, or obtain divisions or cuttings
PLANTING DEPTH:	Just barely cover
SOIL:	Well-drained soil that is not too rich
SUN:	Full sun
SOIL TEMPERATURE:	65° to 70°F (18° to 21°C)
SPACING:	10 to 12 inches (25 to 30 cm) apart
GROWING:	Seedlings need plenty of moisture to thrive, but once plants are established, watering can be tapered off. Transplants or divisions are also a great choice for getting started with oregano, especially if you stumble upon one that you particularly like the flavor of. Oregano prefers a sunny spot with good drainage. Pruning will help the plant become bushy and keep it from getting out of control. At the end of the growing season, cut the plants back to a few inches tall.
HARVEST:	Harvest leaves or whole stems as needed. Use fresh, or dry for longer storage.
CONTAINERS:	Oregano is great for containers.

As a culinary herb, oregano is essential to Mediterranean and Middle Eastern cuisines, as well as those of other places where this herb has spread. While you may be more familiar with its dried counterpart, fresh oregano has a wonderfully robust, earthy flavor that is quite different. When using fresh, add it toward the end of the cooking process.

For growing, look for Greek and Italian varieties. Like other Mediterranean herbs, oregano isn't fussy and will grow well in soil that isn't super fertile. In fact, in richer soils, its flavor may be muted. It's also a perennial in most areas. (Mexican oregano, *Lippa graveolens*, is delicious as well, but botanically it is not a true oregano.)

PARSLEY

Petroselinum crispum

FAMILY:	Apiaceae
SEASON:	Cool weather, spring, fall
PROPAGATION:	Start indoors from seed, buy transplants
PLANTING DEPTH:	¼ to ½ inch (6 to 13 mm)
SOIL:	Well-drained soil with added compost
SUN:	Full sun to part shade
SOIL TEMPERATURE:	65° to 70°F (18° to 21°C)
SPACING:	8 to 10 inches (20 to 25 cm) apart
GROWING:	Parsley takes a while to germinate (14 to 28 days) and then get going as a seedling. Soaking the seeds overnight is said to help accelerate germination. If you find it fussy to grow from seed, buy started plants. For robust growth, make sure to give the plants space and thin them to the recommended spacing. (If you buy transplants, there may be more than one in a pot, so be sure to separate them.) Parsley likes consistent moisture. Mulching can help extend the growing season quite late, as parsley can tolerate a bit of frost. You can also bring parsley indoors and grow it on a windowsill or under grow lights to have a bit of green in the depths of winter.

HARVEST: Harvest leaves from the outside of the plant to allow the smaller inner leaves to mature.

CONTAINERS: Parsley makes a great container plant.

One of the most versatile herbs, parsley is delicious both raw and cooked and can be added to vegetable, meat, and fish dishes; pestos; and even smoothies. You just need to decide if you're Team Curly Leaf or Team Flat-Leaf—I find flat-leaf (Italian) parsley tastier and better from a textural standpoint, but their growing requirements are the same.

A member of the carrot family, parsley is a biennial (flowering in the second year), though most people grow it as an annual because once it flowers, it's too bitter to enjoy.

PEAS

Pisum sativum

FAMILY: Fabaceae

SEASON: Cool weather, spring

PROPAGATION: Sow directly in the garden, start indoors from seed

PLANTING DEPTH: ½ to 1 inch (1.3 to 2.5 cm)

SOIL: Well-drained soil with added compost

SUN: Full sun

SOIL TEMPERATURE: 60° to 70°F (16° to 21°C)

SPACING: 1 to 2 inches (2.5 to 5 cm) apart in rows 18 inches (46 cm) apart

GROWING: Ideally, work extra compost into the bed in the fall before planting and mulch well. It's preferred to sow peas directly in the garden because the plants don't like their roots disturbed, but you can start them indoors to get a head start; just handle the transplants carefully. While peas like cool temps, they don't like soggy soil, so if your spring weather is typically very rainy, raised beds are a great option. Add supports as soon as you plant.

HARVEST: Shell peas and snap peas can be harvested once the pods have filled out—crack a pod open and taste a pea; it will be very sweet. Peas will turn starchy when they are overripe. Snow peas can be harvested as soon as small peas form in the pod.

CONTAINERS: Yes, just add poles or another support.

Peas are one of the great fleeting delicacies of the home garden. They have a short season, are sweetest right after picking, and are unlike anything you can buy in a supermarket because they don't store or travel well. Their arrival also means that spring is finally taking hold and winter has released its grip. Beans (see page 82) have similar cultural requirements, but peas need cooler temperatures to thrive, while beans like warm weather. Like beans, there are pole (or climbing) and bush varieties. Climbing peas, like pole beans (see page 84), will need something to grow on, such as a trellis. Some bush types may benefit from supports as well, depending on how tall they're supposed to get.

There are three types of peas to choose from: Shell peas, or English peas, have an inedible pod from which the peas are removed before cooking or eating. Snap peas, or sugar snap peas, are eaten pod and all. Snow peas, flat pods with very small peas inside, are also eaten pod and all—they're commonly used in stir-fries.

PEPPERS AND CHILES

Capsicum annuum

FAMILY:	Solanaceae
SEASON:	Warm weather, summer
PROPAGATION:	Start indoors from seed
PLANTING DEPTH:	¼ inch (6 mm)
SOIL:	Well-drained soil with added compost
SUN:	Full sun
SOIL TEMPERATURE:	65°F (18°C)
SPACING:	18 inches (46 cm) apart
GROWING:	Pepper seeds prefer warm temperatures to germinate, so place them in a toasty spot, such as on a heat mat. After the plants develop their first set of true leaves (see page 51), you can reduce the temperature. When the night temperatures no longer dip below 50°F (10°C) and the soil temperature is around 65°F (18°C), they can be transplanted to the garden. Avoid overdoing the fertilizer: too much nitrogen can spur lush leaf growth instead of fruit. Instead, a fertilizer with a higher percentage of phosphorus will help encourage flowering and fruiting. While peppers like hot weather, they don't like it too hot (over 90°F/32°C)—or they'll

Peppers and Chiles   135

Veg Out

drop blossoms. Most people grow pepper plants as annuals, but they are perennial. If the plants are still healthy at the end of the growing season, you can dig them up, bring them inside, and return them to the garden the next year.

HARVEST: Harvest peppers as they mature to encourage further growth. The seed packet will indicate the approximate size of the peppers at maturity and will likely specify days to harvest for both green (immature) peppers and ripe peppers.

CONTAINERS: Peppers are ideal for containers.

Flame-red Italian frying peppers. Eggplant-purple bell peppers. Neon-orange chiles. Lime-green wax peppers. Deep green poblanos. Whether you like them sweet or hot—or both!—peppers are a colorful must-have in the garden. The endless varieties to choose from will make you forget what you used to buy at the supermarket. And despite their diversity of shapes, sizes, and heat levels, their growing requirements are pretty much the same!

Peppers are firmly in the warm-weather camp, but you'll need to start thinking about them when summer weather still seems hard to imagine, because they have a long period to maturity. Depending on the length of your growing season, you'll want to start your pepper seeds indoors 8 to 10 weeks before you transplant them.

If you find yourself running out of space in the garden plot, consider containers. Peppers are a superb container plant.

POTATOES

Solanum tuberosum

FAMILY:	Solanaceae
SEASON:	Depends on climate
PROPAGATION:	Direct-sow with seed potatoes
PLANTING DEPTH:	3 inches (8 cm)
SOIL:	Well-drained soil with added compost
SUN:	Full sun
SOIL TEMPERATURE:	55° to 60°F (13° to 16°C)
SPACING:	12 inches (30 cm) apart in rows 36 inches (91 cm) apart
GROWING:	Potatoes are traditionally planted in a trench about 3 inches (8 cm) deep. Plant your seed potato pieces cut side down and sprout side up, and cover with several inches of soil. When the plants are about 6 inches (15 cm) tall, you'll need to begin hilling them up. This essentially means mounding up soil around the plant so that only the top few inches are visible. You'll do this once or twice more as the plant grows, until the hill is about 12 inches (30 cm) tall. While this process might seem a little bit unusual, there's a good reason for it. By hilling the soil, none of the developing potatoes are exposed to the sunlight, which could cause the potatoes to produce a toxic chemical called solanine (the compound that makes potatoes turn green). Potatoes like to stay evenly moist.

Thin-skinned new potatoes (baby potatoes) are a delight and can be harvested for a few weeks after the plants stop flowering. When the main crop of potatoes is almost ready, the foliage will die back. Wait about 2 weeks more before harvesting, which will increase the length of time you can store the potatoes. Dig them up gently, being careful not to pierce or bruise the skin. You may be surprised at how many you've got!

CONTAINERS: Potatoes can be grown in containers or even grow bags. You'll need a large container to leave room for the hilling-up process.

Potatoes were originally domesticated in the Andes. While there are more than four thousand varieties of this root vegetable, not all are available commercially. Still, seed companies offer quite a few options, including varieties in rich jewel tones like red, gold, and purple. As with many garden crops, homegrown potatoes taste so much better than anything you can get at the grocery store, and there are so many flavor nuances and textures.

Potatoes are grown from seed potatoes. To ensure they're disease-free and will sprout, do not use potatoes you've bought in the supermarket. A few days before you plan to plant, cut the seed potatoes into 1- to 1½-inch (2.5 to 4 cm) chunks that have at least one eye (preferably two), and set them aside to heal. (The eyes are the parts that will sprout.)

There are three kinds of potatoes: early, main (or midseason), and late. Early potatoes mature faster but do not store well, so they're great for eating right away. Midseason and late potatoes generally store well. You can choose your varieties depending on the length of the growing season.

Potatoes are a cool-weather crop, and when you plant depends on your climate. In year-round warm climates, you can plant in fall for a winter crop. In climates with hot summers, plant in mid-to-late winter. In cooler climates, plant in early-to-mid spring. Check with fellow gardeners or your local extension office for recommendations.

Potatoes   141

PUMPKINS AND WINTER SQUASH

Cucurbita spp.

FAMILY:	Cucurbitaceae
SEASON:	Warm weather, summer, fall
PROPAGATION:	Sow directly in the garden, start indoors from seed
PLANTING DEPTH:	½ to 1 inch (1.3 to 2.5 cm)
SOIL:	Well-drained soil with plenty of added compost
SUN:	Full sun
SOIL TEMPERATURE:	70°F (21°C) or higher
SPACING:	2 to 3 feet (61 to 91 cm) apart in rows 6 feet/1.8 m (or more, up to 10 feet/3 m) apart, depending on the size of the squash; if growing vertically, this spacing can be reduced. Refer to the seed packet for specific recommendations.
GROWING:	Winter squash need a long, frost-free growing season. Many varieties mature in 95 to 100 days. If you live in an area with a shorter growing season, you can start your seeds indoors. Otherwise, you can sow the seeds directly when the soil is warm enough. If sowing directly, plant the seeds in groups of two to four (several inches apart) and then thin to choose the strongest plant by clipping the seedling off at soil level to avoid disturbing the roots of the

other plants. The plants will need water, and a lot of it, in order to produce, especially while the squash are maturing. Fertilize with seaweed emulsion or a balanced organic fertilizer.

HARVEST: Harvest when the stem starts to dry and become woody and the squash's skin starts to harden. (If you try to nick the skin with your fingernail, you should not be able to pierce it.) The growing instructions may also give other indicators like color or size. Use pruning shears to harvest, leaving a stem 1 to 2 inches (2.5 to 5 cm) long. Handle the squash carefully, because it still needs to be cured for storage; let it cure in a warm area with good air circulation for 7 to 10 days before storing in a cool, dry place.

CONTAINERS: If you're up for a challenge, you can grow squash in containers, but for success, you'll need a very large container and will need to keep up with the watering and fertilizing. Choose bush varieties and smaller squashes, such as acorn and butternut squash.

The term "winter squash" is a bit of a misnomer, because these plants (including pumpkins) are firmly a warm-weather crop. The seeds will rot in cold, wet soil, and the leaves do not tolerate a frost. They are harvested in the autumn, and it's because they can be stored for a long time—into the winter—that they are known as "winter" squash.

In addition to pumpkins for jack-o'-lanterns, this group includes butternut, kabocha, acorn, spaghetti, delicata, potimarron (red kuri), and many other beautiful, diverse varieties to explore. Squash vines are huge (*huge!*) and will sprawl all over (sometimes 20 feet/6 m or longer), so planting them on the edge of your garden is recommended. Alternatively, if space is limited, you can grow them vertically and support the growing fruits with a mesh sling or other type of support. Pumpkins and winter squash are great to grow with children because the seeds are big and easy for them to plant, and it's fun to watch the rapid growth of the plant and development of the fruit.

Squash plants produce both male and female flowers. The male flowers have a thin stem, and the female flowers have a swollen base. The flowers must be open at the same time to be pollinated in order for fruit to develop. At the beginning of the growing season, it's common for the plant to produce more male flowers, but this will improve as the season progresses. If pollination does not occur due to a lack of pollinators, plants can be hand-pollinated by transferring the pollen from the anther of the male flower to the stigma of the female flower. This can be done with a cotton swab or brush, or by removing the male flower and physically brushing the anther against the stigma of the female flower.

RADISHES

Raphanus sativus

FAMILY:	Brassicaceae
SEASON:	Cool weather, spring, fall
PROPAGATION:	Sow directly in the garden
PLANTING DEPTH:	½ inch (1.3 cm)
SOIL:	Well-drained soil with added compost or leaf mold
SUN:	Full sun
SOIL TEMPERATURE:	45° to 85°F (7° to 29°C)
SPACING:	Small radishes: 1 to 2 inches (2.5 to 5 cm) apart in rows 12 inches (30 cm) apart; large radishes (e.g., daikon): 6 inches (15 cm) apart in rows 12 to 18 inches (30 to 46 cm) apart
GROWING:	Radishes don't need much in the way of help except consistently moist, cool soil and proper spacing. Too much nitrogen can lead to lush leaves and puny roots, so go easy with the fertilizer. Daikon, Korean, and other specialty radishes take longer to mature than round radishes because of their larger size. For a steady harvest, plant a modest amount every 7 to 10 days during the spring, early summer, and fall. In hot weather, radishes will bolt, taste extra spicy, and have a tough texture.

HARVEST: Harvest promptly when the radishes reach the diameter indicated on the seed packet. For small radishes, this is usually about an inch (2.5 cm) across. You may need to brush aside some soil or even pull one out to check. Don't leave them in the ground too long because they will turn bitter.

CONTAINERS: Radishes grow well in containers.

Radishes are a fun, quick, cool-weather crop that you can squeeze in just about anywhere, even under other crops that take a longer time to mature, such as tomatoes, peppers, and cucumbers; the radishes will be long gone by the time the other crop is ready. Some varieties mature in just 21 days! If you have kids, growing radishes can be a great way to get them interested in the garden, because they don't have to wait long to see results.

Try branching out beyond the little red radishes you find at the grocery store. Pink-and-white french breakfast radishes, watermelon radishes (which have green skin and a deep-pink interior), and ice-white daikons are just a few options to consider.

ROSEMARY

Rosmarinus officinalis

FAMILY:	Lamiaceae
SEASON:	n/a
PROPAGATION:	Obtain cuttings, buy started plants
PLANTING DEPTH:	n/a
SOIL:	Very well-drained soil
SUN:	Full sun
SOIL TEMPERATURE:	n/a
SPACING:	24 to 36 inches (61 to 91 cm) apart
GROWING:	Established rosemary plants are drought tolerant. Avoid planting in heavy clay soils. In cooler climates, you can bring rosemary indoors for the winter.
HARVEST:	Harvest leaves as needed.
CONTAINERS:	Rosemary is an ideal container plant.

A powerfully scented herb redolent of resin and pine, rosemary is as at home tossed with roasted potatoes as it is with grilled lamb. Sprinkle it on focaccia or add it to cocktails as a garnish to infuse the drink with its aroma.

Rosemary is a perennial shrub in warmer climates and can be trimmed as a hedge. Like most Mediterranean herbs, it wants very well-drained soil and dislikes soggy, cold feet.

Rosemary is very challenging to grow from seed, so either buy started plants or get cuttings from a fellow gardener.

SAGE

Salvia officinalis

FAMILY:	Lamiaceae
SEASON:	n/a
PROPAGATION:	Buy started plants, start indoors from seed, sow directly in the garden
PLANTING DEPTH:	¼ inch (6 mm)
SOIL:	Very well-drained soil
SUN:	Full sun to part shade (in hot climates)
SOIL TEMPERATURE:	65° to 85°F (18° to 29°C)
SPACING:	18 to 30 inches (46 to 76 cm) apart
GROWING:	Though sage is easy to grow from seed, it takes 2 years to fully establish, so consider buying started plants instead of planting seeds (see harvest suggestions). Established sage plants are drought tolerant. Avoid planting in heavy, clay soils. Cut woody growth back in the spring, and replace plants every 3 to 4 years.
HARVEST:	If you do grow from seed, harvest modestly the first year. Sage leaves can be used fresh, or you can dry them for longer storage.
CONTAINERS:	Sage grows well in containers.

With soft gray-green leaves and a woodsy, citrusy scent, sage is an attractive herb that is essential for stuffing, sausages, and other savory dishes. Try crisping up sage leaves in brown butter and tossing with pasta, vegetables, or potatoes. In the garden, sage is a perennial in most climates and is easy to grow, particularly if you buy started plants. As a Mediterranean herb, it wants very well-drained soil.

Sage

SCALLIONS
(GREEN ONIONS)

Allium fistulosum

FAMILY:	Amaryllidaceae
SEASON:	n/a
PROPAGATION:	Start indoors from seed, sow directly in the garden, use divisions
PLANTING DEPTH:	¼ inch (6 mm)
SOIL:	Well-drained soil with added compost
SUN:	Full sun
SOIL TEMPERATURE:	45° to 75°F (7° to 24°C)
SPACING:	¼ to ½ inch (6 to 13 mm) apart in rows 12 inches (30 cm) apart
GROWING:	Growing scallions is relatively simple. Keep the area well weeded and ensure consistent moisture.
HARVEST:	Harvest when the scallions reach the desired size.
CONTAINERS:	Scallions are easy to grow in a container. You can even regrow cut scallions.

For many, scallions (or green onions) are essential in the kitchen, and are used just as you would many herbs. They're great in stir-fries and tacos, sprinkled on soups, layered in scallion pancakes (of course!), mixed into cornbread batter. . . . Even though it's so easy to just pick up a bunch of scallions at the grocery store, you'll find that growing them yourself is really worth it for the incomparable flavor. And for new gardeners, scallions are an easy alternative to bulbing onions. You don't have to worry about day-length requirements or decide whether you're growing from plants, sets, or seeds—or even understand what that means. Plus, they mature in about half the time. In seed catalogs, you'll find scallions listed as "bunching onions." Because they're so hardy, you might even have scallions through winter if you live in a mild climate.

SPINACH

Spinacia oleracea

FAMILY:	Amaranthaceae
SEASON:	Cool weather, early spring, fall, winter
PROPAGATION:	Sow directly in the garden (seedlings are difficult to transplant)
PLANTING DEPTH:	½ inch (1.3 cm)
SOIL:	Well-drained soil with added compost
SUN:	Full sun to part shade
SOIL TEMPERATURE:	45° to 70°F (7° to 21°C)
SPACING:	Baby spinach: 3 inches (8 cm) apart; full-size spinach: 6 inches (15 cm) apart
GROWING:	Sow every 7 to 10 days for a continuous harvest. Ensure that the plants receive consistent water, and mulch to keep the soil temperature cool. As the days lengthen and warm, providing some shade can help prolong the growing season.
HARVEST:	Harvest baby spinach as soon as the leaves reach the desired size, cutting leaves from the outside of the plant first to allow the inner leaves time to mature. You can also harvest the entire plant at maturity.
CONTAINERS:	Spinach can be grown in a container at least 10 inches (25 cm) deep.

Spinach likes to play it cool, really cool. It's one of the earliest spring vegetables and can be grown in fall and into winter, as it can tolerate a bit of frost. On the other hand, warm temperatures and long days cause it to bolt. Fortunately, it matures quite quickly, with some varieties ready to clip for baby greens in 25 days, so even if you have a short window for growing it, you should be able to get in a good harvest. You can choose between smooth-leaf and savoyed-leaf (wrinkled) varieties. For a spinach alternative in the hottest days of summer, try red-leaf amaranth (a fellow member of the amaranth family; see page 76) or Malabar spinach (*Basella alba*), a tropical vining plant with a somewhat similar flavor.

If you've bought bunches of supermarket spinach before, you might think it needs sandy soil because it's usually covered in it, but in fact it's quite adaptable to a range of soil conditions. It does, however, prefer a pH that is close to neutral.

SWEET POTATOES

Ipomoea batatas

FAMILY:	Convolvulaceae
SEASON:	Warm weather, summer
PROPAGATION:	Slips (see headnote)
PLANTING DEPTH:	4 to 6 inches (10 to 15 cm; see Growing)
SOIL:	Very well-drained soil with added compost
SUN:	Full sun
SOIL TEMPERATURE:	60°F (16°C) or higher
SPACING:	12 to 18 inches (30 to 46 cm) apart in rows 3 to 5 feet (about 1 to 1.5 m) apart
GROWING:	Because these are tropical plants, the soil temperature must be 60°F (15°C) or higher when you plant your slips. (Black plastic mulch can be used to help warm the soil faster.) Plant the slips deep enough that the roots are covered, 4 to 6 inches (10 to 15 cm) deep. Water the slips well as soon as they go into the ground and for the next week, until the plants have become established. Provide a high-phosphorus fertilizer. Too much nitrogen will encourage leafy growth at the expense of tuber development. When temperatures are particularly hot and dry, ensure the plants get sufficient water.
HARVEST:	When the sweet potatoes are ready, the leaves will start to turn yellow. Dig them up carefully so as not to bruise them, which affects their

storage potential. All sweet potatoes should be harvested before the first frost. Just brush off the dirt; they should not be washed yet. To cure them for storage, place them in a warm, airy location (around 85°F/29°C) with high humidity for 7 to 10 days.

CONTAINERS: Choose bush varieties like Bush Porto Rico.

Potatoes, as you may recall from page 138, are members of the nightshade family, a group that includes tomatoes, eggplants, tomatillos, and other vegetables. While sweet potatoes might look potato-like, they're not related in the slightest. Instead, they come from the morning glory family. Native to tropical zones of the Americas, sweet potatoes require a long, hot growing season and plenty of sun, but some varieties with a shorter period to maturity can be grown in cooler climates.

Sweet potatoes are not grown from seed but from rooted cuttings called slips, which you can purchase through a seed company or local nursery. If you have a shorter growing season, choose a variety appropriate for your conditions (for example, Beauregard matures in 90 days). In addition to warmth, sweet potatoes like plenty of sunshine and water and, as a vining plant, need plenty of room to spread.

SWISS CHARD

Beta vulgaris ssp. *cicla*

FAMILY:	Amaranthaceae
SEASON:	Cool weather, spring, fall
PROPAGATION:	Start indoors, sow directly
PLANTING DEPTH:	½ inch (1.3 cm)
SOIL:	Well-drained soil with added compost
SUN:	Full sun to part shade
SOIL TEMPERATURE:	45° to 85°F (7° to 29°C)
SPACING:	Baby greens, 1 inch (2.5 cm) apart; full-size plants, 4 to 6 inches (10 to 15 cm) apart
GROWING:	Swiss chard is easy to grow. You can sow it directly throughout the spring and fall growing seasons, staggering the planting for a consistent harvest. Ensure consistent watering and mulch to extend the growing season, both into summer and into the winter.
HARVEST:	Baby greens can be snipped when they reach the desired size, 3 to 5 inches (8 to 13 cm). Harvest full-size leaves (10 to 12 inches/25 to 30 cm long) from the outside of the plant first to give the inner leaves time to mature.
CONTAINERS:	Yes; chard can also be grown on a sunny windowsill.

Swiss chard looks a bit like kale, but it is a member of the amaranth family and of the same genus and species as beets, while kale is a brassica (in the same group as broccoli and cabbage). It has beautiful savoyed (ruffled) leaves, and some varieties have rainbow-colored stems. If you don't like beets, though, you probably won't like Swiss chard either, because it also contains the compound geosmin (see page 87). Baby chard, however, might be more to your liking, especially mixed with other baby greens. In addition to being a powerhouse in the nutrition department, it's also quite tolerant to cold weather and can even tolerate some frost.

THYME

Thymus vulgaris

FAMILY:	Lamiaceae
SEASON:	n/a
PROPAGATION:	Established plants, divisions, or cuttings
PLANTING DEPTH:	n/a
SOIL:	Well-drained loose soil
SUN:	Full sun
SOIL TEMPERATURE:	n/a
SPACING:	8 to 12 inches (20 to 30 cm)
GROWING:	Transplant thyme to the garden after the last frost. It does not like heavy clay soils, so amend the soil to add extra drainage. It will grow in rocky soil, too, as long as it's sunny, so it's a good choice for a spot that isn't good for much else. Thyme is not fussy but does not like to stay wet for long, which can cause root rot. Prune as needed to remove woody growth, limit spread, and stimulate new growth. Like sage (see page 150), the plants will need to be replaced every few years.
HARVEST:	Harvest sprigs as needed. They can be used fresh or hung to dry.
CONTAINERS:	Thyme grows well in containers.

A perennial Mediterranean herb, thyme has an earthy, minty flavor that makes it perfect with roast chicken or potatoes, in pan sauces, and more. It's also an essential ingredient in many spice mixes, including Jamaican jerk seasoning. While you can experiment with growing thyme from seed, it's challenging; it takes a while to get going and tends to stay quite scraggly for a while. Instead, buy established plants, or obtain divisions or cuttings from a friend. Thyme doesn't need especially fertile soil or careful attention. It likes sunny, dry conditions and excellent drainage.

Some varieties of thyme are used ornamentally. Creeping thyme, also known as mother-of-thyme, is an attractive ground cover in rock gardens, on pavers, and in borders. Its beautiful flowers attract bees. Culinary thyme, by contrast, has an upright growth pattern and becomes woody over time. Another thyme to consider growing for culinary use is lemon thyme (*Thymus citriodorus*). While lemon thyme was once thought to be a hybrid of *T. vulgaris*, it's now considered its own species.

TOMATOES

Solanum lycopersicum

FAMILY:	Solanaceae
SEASON:	Warm weather, summer
PROPAGATION:	Start indoors from seed, buy transplants
PLANTING DEPTH:	¼ inch (6 mm)
SOIL:	Light, well-drained soil with added compost and tomato fertilizer
SUN:	Full sun
SOIL TEMPERATURE:	65° to 70°F (18° to 21°C)
SPACING:	Determinate tomatoes: 12 to 24 inches (30 to 61 cm); indeterminate tomatoes: 24 to 36 inches (61 to 91 cm)
GROWING:	You can grow tomatoes from seed or buy plants, but buying plants may be easier, especially for new gardeners who want fewer variables to deal with. A good nursery will likely have a broad variety of options for you to choose from, including heirlooms, but they will not have the seemingly endless choices of a seed catalog. Ensure the seedlings you choose look healthy and vigorous, are compact for their size (not leggy and stretched out in appearance), and have no open flowers. When transplanting your seedlings, dig a hole deep enough that only the top 4 to 5 inches (10 to 13 cm) of the plant are aboveground. Remove the bottom few leaves (from the part of the stem that will be

underground). Roots will develop from the underground part of the stem. Add stakes or tomato cages to support the tomatoes as they grow; you will need to tie them in as they get larger. To help the plant concentrate its energy on maturing fruit and keep it from getting too unruly as it grows, pinch off the little shoots (called suckers) that appear between the main plant stem and a branch. Tomatoes like consistent, deep moisture but don't like sitting in soggy soil.

ADDITIONAL TIPS: Blossom-end rot is caused by a calcium deficiency and will manifest itself as a dark soggy spot on the bottom of the tomato. If this occurs, remove any affected tomatoes, ensure that the plant isn't getting too soggy or too dry (consistent watering is best), and avoid high-nitrogen fertilizers. To help avoid blight, which can quickly kill a tomato plant, ensure proper spacing, stake tomatoes, and water only the soil (avoid splashing the leaves). Plants with blight must be destroyed. If blossoms drop from the plant, temperatures may be too hot, or there might not be enough pollinators in your garden.

HARVEST: Harvest tomatoes when they have turned the right color (red, yellow, orange, etc.) but are still firm. It's perfectly fine if they are still yellow at the top. Tomatoes will mature off the vine as well, so if a frost threatens, you can harvest the remaining tomatoes and let them ripen on the kitchen counter. You can also ripen tomatoes outside, out of direct sunlight, like on a bench in the shade.

CONTAINERS: Try determinate varieties, cherry tomatoes, dwarf, or micro-dwarf tomatoes. Micro-dwarf varieties can also be grown indoors under grow lights. (Renaissance Farms, renaissancefarms.org, is a great source of micro-dwarf varieties.)

Veg Out

For many, tomatoes are the sine qua non of the garden, the must-have, never-be-without-it plant. And why not? They're one of the most beloved garden crops, whether eaten raw or cooked, and few things get a gardener's heart beating faster than a good tomato harvest. They come in almost every color of the rainbow, the heirlooms have perfectly imperfect shapes, and many have quirky names like Mortgage Lifter, Pork Chop, and Pink Berkeley Tie-Dye. Some of my favorite heirlooms include Green Zebra, which as the name suggests, has zebra-striped green skin; Garden Peach, which is fuzzy like a peach; and Black Krim, a juicy beefsteak heirloom tomato.

And yet . . . almost every beginning gardener wants to grow tomatoes, and almost every gardener—regardless of experience—has struggled with growing tomatoes and will struggle again. The blossoms drop off, the plant gets a blight, the tomatoes are malformed, the leaves are covered in whiteflies, or you simply just don't get many tomatoes for all the effort and fussing you heap upon the plants. So many things can go wrong, and sometimes, it's just a bad year. I once grew a mammoth Black Krim plant that produced exactly one perfect tomato. It happens.

There's only so much we can control. As Jane Perrone, host of the houseplant podcast *On the Ledge*, has said, "For some reason, people often decide that they want to grow vegetables for the very first time, and tomatoes are the things that they pick to grow, which is a bit like deciding you're going to get into cooking and attempting a Heston Blumenthal recipe as your first recipe, because tomatoes are not the easiest thing in the world to grow."

That said, I don't want to dissuade you from growing tomatoes. You should grow them. I just want to manage your expectations and let you know that if you don't get the kind of harvest you were expecting, it's almost certainly not your fault. (And here's a little secret: cherry tomatoes are easier.)

Tomatoes have two main growing styles: determinate and indeterminate. Determinate tomatoes are bush-style plants (something we saw with beans and cucumbers and a few other plants), and they mature their fruit during a window of a few weeks. Because of their smaller size, this kind is ideal for containers, and you can often get away with not staking or caging them. If this is your first time growing tomatoes, I would recommend a determinate variety, particularly a cherry tomato. Indeterminate tomatoes are large vining plants, and will continue to produce throughout the growing season. You will need to stake or cage these plants.

ZUCCHINI

Cucurbita pepo

FAMILY:	Cucurbitaceae
SEASON:	Warm weather, summer
PROPAGATION:	Sow directly, start indoors
PLANTING DEPTH:	¾ to 1 inch (2 to 2.5 cm)
SOIL:	Well-drained soil with added compost and leaf mold
SUN:	Full sun
SOIL TEMPERATURE:	85°F (29°C)
SPACING:	24 inches (61 cm) apart in rows 60 to 72 inches (1.5 to 1.8 m) apart
GROWING:	Direct-sowing summer squash is recommended because they don't like their roots disturbed, but you can start them indoors. Ensure consistent, deep watering, especially when the fruits are forming. Mulch can help maintain moisture. If some of the early squash are misshapen or blacken, it's not an indication that you've done something wrong; the cause is usually lack of pollination. As the plant begins to produce more female flowers, this should improve. If not, you can hand-pollinate the flowers (see page 144).
HARVEST:	Harvest when the zucchini is 6 to 8 inches (15 to 20 cm) long, depending on the variety. When it comes to zucchini, bigger is not better in terms of flavor. Large zucchini can be a bit bitter and watery

Zucchini 167

because they develop large seeds. Male blossoms have a long, thin stem (while female blossoms have a swollen base) and can be harvested when they are fully open.

CONTAINERS: Choose bush varieties.

The first question you need to ask yourself before growing zucchini is, "Do I like zucchini?" If the answer is no or sorta, then move on to something else, because zucchini is notorious for being one of the most prolific garden plants, supplying you with more zucchini than you can possibly (or want to) eat. And just when you think you've found them all . . . no, wait, you missed one, and now it's the length of your forearm. If you like them, then I say go for it, but limit the number of plants. The nice bonus of zucchini is the edible flowers, which can be stuffed, battered, and fried—Costata Romanesco is an heirloom variety that produces nice flowers and tasty striped squash.

Zucchini are considered summer squash because they are harvested in the summer, have thin skin, and do not store well (unlike winter squash; see page 142), but their growing needs are quite similar to those of winter squash. They need very fertile soil (add lots of compost), lots of water, and perhaps some supplemental seaweed emulsion or balanced fertilizer. Other summer squash, such as pattypan and yellow squash, can be grown the same way.

BIBLIOGRAPHY
AND FURTHER READING

BBC Gardeners' World Magazine. "Find Out Your Soil Type." GardenersWorld.com, May 11, 2019. gardenersworld.com/plants/find-out-your-soil-type.

Bernitz, Nate. "Low and No-Till Gardening." University of New Hampshire Extension, October 16, 2020. https://extension.unh.edu/blog/2020/10/low-no-till-gardening.

Byron, Morgan A., and Jennifer L. Gillett-Kaufman. "Tomato Hornworm." Entomology and Nematology Department, University of Florida, January 2018. https://entnemdept.ufl.edu/creatures/FIELD/hornworm.htm.

"Composting for Beginners." Better Homes and Gardens. YouTube, November 3, 2017. youtube.com/watch?v=bGRunDez1j4.

Don, Monty. *The Complete Gardener.* New York: DK, 2021.

Dowding, Charles. "Start Out No Dig, One Method with Cardboard and Compost." YouTube, March 29, 2020. youtube.com/watch?v=0LH6-w57Slw.

Doucleff, Michaeleen. "Love to Hate Cilantro? It's in Your Genes and Maybe, in Your Head." NPR, September 14, 2012. npr.org/sections/thesalt/2012/09/14/161057954/love-to-hate-cilantro-its-in-your-genes-and-maybe-in-your-head.

Erler, Emma. "What Should Neem Be Used for on Plants?" University of New Hampshire Extension, January 22, 2020. https://extension.unh.edu/blog/2020/01/what-should-neem-be-used-plants.

Gevens, Amanda, Anna Seidl, and Brian Hudelson. "Late Blight." Wisconsin Horticulture–Division of Extension, June 16, 2017. https://hort.extension.wisc.edu/articles/late-blight.

Hahn, Jeffrey et al. "Flea Beetles in Home Gardens." University of Minnesota Extension. https://extension.umn.edu/yard-and-garden-insects/flea-beetles.

Hahn, Jeffrey, and Suzanne Wold-Burkness. "Tomato Hornworms in Home Gardens." University of Minnesota Extension. https://extension.umn.edu/yard-and-garden-insects/tomato-hornworms.

———. "Squash Bugs in Home Gardens." University of Minnesota Extension. https://extension.umn.edu/fruit-and-vegetable-insects/squash-bugs.

"How to Identify, Control, and Prevent Mosaic Viruses." Almanac.com. almanac.com/pest/mosaic-viruses.

Klopp, Glenn, and Chip Tynan. "Hand Pollination of Squash and Pumpkins." Missouri Botanic Garden. missouribotanicalgarden.org/gardens-gardening/your-garden/help-for-the-home-gardener/advice-tips-resources/visual-guides/pollination-of-squash-and-pumpkins.aspx.

"Leaf Miners." PennState Extension, updated May 28, 2015. https://extension.psu.edu/leaf-miners.

Maher, Lynn, and Irwin L. Goldman. "Endogenous Production of Geosmin in Table Beet." *HortScience* 53, no. 1 (January 2018). https://journals.ashs.org/hortsci/view/journals/hortsci/53/1/article-p67.xml.

Meadows, Inga. "Early Blight of Tomato." NC State Extension, December 11, 2015. https://content.ces.ncsu.edu/early-blight-of-tomato.

"Mexican Bean Beetle." Purdue University Field Crops IPM. https://extension.entm.purdue.edu/fieldcropsipm/insects/mexican-bean-beetle.php.

"Mexican Bean Beetle—Vegetables." University of Maryland Extension, updated September 30, 2021. https://extension.umd.edu/resource/mexican-bean-beetle-vegetables.

Nardozzi, Charlie. *Vegetable Gardening for Dummies*, 2nd ed. Hoboken, NJ: Wiley, 2009.

The Old Farmer's Almanac. *Vegetable Gardener's Handbook*. Dublin, NH: Yankee Publishing, 2019.

"The Old Farmer's Almanac Companion Planting Guide." The Old Farmer's Almanac, January 22, 2022. almanac.com/companion-planting-guide-vegetables.

Perrone, Jane. "Episode 150: Introducing the *On the Ledge* Manifesto." *On the Ledge*, August 7, 2020. janeperrone.com/on-the-ledge/2020/7/19/episode-150-the-on-the-ledge-manifesto.

"Potato Facts and Figures." CIP International Potato Center. https://cipotato.org/potato/potato -facts-and-figures.

Smith, Edward C. *The Vegetable Gardener's Bible*. North Adams, MA: Storey Publishing, 2009.

"Soil: Understanding pH and Testing Soil." Royal Horticultural Society. rhs.org.uk/soil-composts -mulches/ph-and-testing-soil.

"Soil Types." Royal Horticultural Society. rhs.org.uk/soil-composts-mulches/soil-types.

Sweetser, Robin. "What Is Diatomaceous Earth?" The Old Farmer's Almanac, July 15, 2020. almanac.com/what-diatomaceous-earth.

"Treated Seeds." National Pesticide Information Center, updated January 28, 2020. http://npic .orst.edu/ingred/ptype/treated-seed.html.

"Weed Control." Circular 1027-13. University of Georgia Extension. Reviewed September 13, 2019. https://extension.uga.edu/publications/detail.html?number=C1027-13.

"What's the Difference? Open-Pollinated, Heirloom, and Hybrid Seeds." Seed Savers Exchange, May 12, 2012. https://blog.seedsavers.org/blog/open-pollinated-heirloom-and-hybrid-seeds.

Wong, James. *How to Eat Better*. New York: Sterling Epicure, 2018.

RESOURCES

Planting Guides
The Old Farmer's Almanac

almanac.com/gardening/frostdates

Search for first and last frost dates by ZIP code or postal code. Readers outside the US and Canada should search locally.

almanac.com/gardening/planting-calendar

For approximate dates of what to plant when (including when to start seeds, transplant seedlings, or direct-sow into the garden), visit the planting calendar and enter your ZIP code or postal code. Readers outside the US and Canada should search locally.

Grow Lights
AeroGarden

aerogarden.com

AeroGarden may be best known for selling countertop gardens, but they also sell grow lights on their website. For beginners, the adjustable-height grow light panel is a great place to start.

Spider Farmer

spider-farmer.com

Easy-to-set-up grow lights that can be used for seed starting and even growing indoors from seed to harvest.

Seed Companies

Baker Creek Heirloom Seeds

rareseeds.com

A stunning variety of heirloom seeds and a beautiful annual catalog.

Johnny's Selected Seeds

johnnyseeds.com

A wide variety of both hybrid and heirloom seeds, in addition to tools and supplies.

Kitazawa Seed Co.

kitazawaseed.com

An excellent source for Asian vegetable and herb seeds.

Renaissance Farms

renaissancefarms.org

A small company focused on heirloom and open-pollinated tomato seeds, including micro-dwarf varieties that are ideal for small containers and even indoor growing (under lights).

Southern Exposure Seed Exchange

southernexposure.com

Promotes seed saving and seed exchange. An excellent variety of heirloom and open-pollinated varieties, with a specialization in varieties that grow well in warmer climates.

ACKNOWLEDGMENTS

A book always requires the work of many talented people to shape it into what you hold in your hand. Elysia Liang, the acquiring editor, proposed the concept and provided feedback on the original structure. Jessica Firger later took the helm, editing the manuscript and helping me to clarify and better explain concepts throughout. Thanks, Jess, for making everything so easy. Copyeditor Ivy McFadden did a fantastic job tightening and sharpening my prose. Thanks also to the project editor, Hannah Reich; interior designer, Christine Heun; cover designer, Jo Obarowski; and to everyone else at Union Square & Co. for their hard work and commitment. Thanks especially to my mom for instilling a love of plants, gardening, and food and to my husband for his love and support.

IMAGE CREDITS

Alamy: Felix Choo: 62; Clarence Holmes Wildlife: 68; Przemyslaw Klos: 12

Courtesy of Shannon Cowan/Eartheasy: 17, 18 top and middle

Getty Images: *E+*: johnnyscriv: 141; Jun Shang: 139; YinYang: 68 (Japanese beetle); zoranm: 124; *EyeEm:* Stephen Piggott: 107; *iStock/Getty Images Plus:* abadonian: 66; AHPhotoswpg: 109; ajt: 69 (slub); Bouillante: 38; CatMiche: 135; chuyu: 67; coramueller: 93; del-mar: 55; dianazh: 149; ElenaGa: 99; Floortje: 54; Geo-grafika: x; Rhitesh Ghosh: 69 (Mexican bean beetle): 69; GlobalP: 67; Maksims Grigorjevs: 147; hamikus: 161; Olena Hyria: 133; JAH: 85; Jurgute: 20; Chris Leaver: 83; letterberry: 79; MartaJonina: 129; mtreasure: 60; Nikolaeva Elena: 97; Marianne Pfeil: 159; sanddebeautheil: 23 middle; Peter Shaw: 87; Aleksandr Silchenko: 136; slowmotiongli: 81; SondraP: 103; therry: 53; Vaivirga: 155; Sandra Westermann: 34; y-studio: 111; zlikovec: 22 bottom; *Moment:* Christina Gray: 68 (cucumber beetle); Roberto Machado Noa: 127

Sarah Jun, © Union Square and Co., LLC: vi, viii, ix, 49, back endpaper

Shutterstock.com: Adisa: 54 (trowel); AJCespedes: 22 top; Sergiy Akhundov: 157; Andrey_Kuzmin: 54 (hose); Tatyana Andreyeva: 22 middle; Anastassiiya Bezhekeneva: 28; CorneliaP: 153; ElephantCastle: 54 (rake); Maria Eveyeva: 33; Flower Studio: 52 (shovel); D. Kucharski K. Kucharska: 69 (leaf miner); Deyan Georgiev: 18 bottom; EkaterinaShcherbakova: 143; encierro: 116; gibleho: 23 bottom; jeff gynane: 123; Alison Hancock: 39 bottom; Jamie Hooper: 43; Jamroen_Photo Background: 54 (gardening scissors); jgolby: 26; JoannaTkaczuk: 119; Jukov studio: 8; Kurit afshen: 70 (squash bug); Eldred Lim: 23 top; locote: 54 (watering can); Lunx: 52 (hoe); Paul MacGuire: 163; Max_55: front endpaper; MNStudio: 145; Nadrutda: 101; Kate Nag: 55 (kneeling pad); NataliaL: 115; New Africa: 55 (wheelbarrow, gloves); Nigel M Openshaw: 91; Rtimages: 52 (spade); Svetlana Monyakova: vii; pavla: 131; Peter Turner Photography: 39 top; pics five: 55 (board); Stephen Plaster: 121; Protasov AN: 71; SebastianO Photography: 15; Shyamalamuralinath: 113; Benjamin Simeneta: 70 (hornworm); Stanslav71: 41; superwhite: 95; sutlafk: 105; Diana Taliun: 151; Gert-Jan van Vliet: 89; Sheryl Watson: 167; Vadym Zaitsev: 52 (spading fork), 58; Zolnierek: 74

Stock Food: ©Chris Schäfer: v

Stocksy United: ©MaaHoo Studio: 2; ©Helen Rushbrook: 172

INDEX

Note: Page numbers in **bold** indicate plant profiles.

ABOUT THE AUTHOR

Heather Rodino is the author of *How to Houseplant*
and several other books. An editor and writer, she has
worked in publishing for more than two decades.
She lives in San Juan, Puerto Rico, where she is
fortunate to be able to garden year-round.